Practical OneOps

Implement DevOps with ease

Nilesh Nimkar

BIRMINGHAM - MUMBAI

Practical OneOps

First published: April 2017

Production reference: 1070417

Published by Packt Publishing Ltd.
Livery Place
35 Livery Street
Birmingham
B3 2PB, UK.
ISBN 978-1-78646-199-5

www.packtpub.com

Credits

Author
Nilesh Nimkar

Reviewer
Andy Cohan

Commissioning Editor
Pratik Shah

Acquisition Editor
Vijin Boricha

Content Development Editor
Abhishek Jadhav

Technical Editor
Aditya Khadye

Copy Editors
Dipti Mankame
Safis Editing

Project Coordinator
Judie Jose

Proofreader
Safis Editing

Indexer
Pratik Shirodkar

Graphics
Kirk D'Penha

Production Coordinator
Shantanu Zagade

About the Author

Nilesh Nimkar has 18 years of experience in the IT industry, where he worked as a Release Manager for 13 years with the world's top banks, hedge funds, and data providers, such as Interactive Data, Deutsche Bank, Bridgewater Associates, Barclays, Bank of America, Merrill Lynch, UBS, and Oracle.

During his time at various banks and hedge funds, he was involved in various large-scale automation projects.

He likes to play with cloud and orchestration technologies, such as OpenStack, Docker, and Vagrant. He likes to read through code and reverse-engineer products. He also has a Master's degree in Information Systems from the University of Phoenix and a Bachelor of Science (physics) from the University of Mumbai. He is a certified Financial Information Associate, Mongo DBA, Mongo Developer, Oracle DBA, and Hadoop Admin.

I would like to thank my wife and daughter for putting up with my late nights working on the book. I would like to thank my mom who instilled in me a love for reading. A big thanks to Vijin and Abhishek from Packt, without whom this book would not have seen the light of the day.

Finally, thanks to the team at Walmartlabs for releasing an excellent product as open source, being patient with me, and answering my endless stream of questions.

About the Reviewer

Andy Cohan is a seasoned systems architect, developer, and leader with 30 years of experience in designing and building business information systems. He currently leads the Eastern region for Avalon Consulting, LLC, a big data and digital transformation firm based near Dallas, TX.

www.PacktPub.com

For support files and downloads related to your book, please visit www.PacktPub.com.

Did you know that Packt offers eBook versions of every book published, with PDF and ePub files available? You can upgrade to the eBook version at www.PacktPub.com and as a print book customer, you are entitled to a discount on the eBook copy. Get in touch with us at service@packtpub.com for more details.

At www.PacktPub.com, you can also read a collection of free technical articles, sign up for a range of free newsletters and receive exclusive discounts and offers on Packt books and eBooks.

https://www.packtpub.com/mapt

Get the most in-demand software skills with Mapt. Mapt gives you full access to all Packt books and video courses, as well as industry-leading tools to help you plan your personal development and advance your career.

Why subscribe?

- Fully searchable across every book published by Packt
- Copy and paste, print, and bookmark content
- On demand and accessible via a web browser

Customer Feedback

Thanks for purchasing this Packt book. At Packt, quality is at the heart of our editorial process. To help us improve, please leave us an honest review on this book's Amazon page at https://www.amazon.com/dp/1786461994.

If you'd like to join our team of regular reviewers, you can e-mail us at customerreviews@packtpub.com. We award our regular reviewers with free eBooks and videos in exchange for their valuable feedback. Help us be relentless in improving our products!

Table of Contents

Preface

OneOps is complex yet easy to use PaaS Application Lifecycle Management software built by Walmart Labs, which is owned by Walmart. Walmart uses OneOps to manage its e-commerce infrastructure sites, such as `walmart.com` and Sam's Club. However, before switching to OneOps any updates to Walmart's infrastructure were huge tasks and required complex planning and execution. Updates were done every two months, required hundreds of manual steps and considerable resources, and left a lot of room for errors. This also made testing quite difficult. This is common scenario in a lot of organizations where legacy products can run and become bloated and monolithic to the point of being unmanageable. Organizations become complacent and are either afraid of or are resistant to change, opting instead to maintain the status quo, most of the time at a terrible cost to productivity. This all started to change with the advent of DevOps. While DevOps is about fostering a cooperative culture among teams, it begins by giving increased control to developers over their own applications. DevOps is also about enabling rapid changes across all environments at the speed of development. Walmart used OneOps to implement the DevOps paradigm, allowing them to move from their monolithic bi-monthly deployments to rapidly evolving 1000 deployments per day across their global e-commerce infrastructure. OneOps abstracts the underlying cloud infrastructure from the developers irrespective of the tools and technologies they use. OneOps also allows developers to define their application along with the infrastructure requirements in a easy to use generic GUI, which it then translates to whichever cloud the application gets deployed to. This avoids being locked in to a cloud vendor, allowing companies to benefit from having redundancies for their applications and to also benefit from competitive cloud vendor technologies and pricing. OneOps also provides services such as monitoring, auto-scaling, and auto-repair for deployed applications. And best of all, it's available for free under open source.

In this book, we will explore the practical aspects of OneOps from the point of view of a DevOps engineer. Irrespective of whether you have been asked to evaluate OneOps as a potential technology to implement as an abstraction on your cloud infrastructure or if you are doing a enterprise deployment of OneOps, you will find something useful in this book. We will start with the basics such as various ways of installing a test installation of OneOps. We will then look at the architecture of OneOps and the various components that comprise the backend. We will then see how to create and deploy and assembly. We will also look at a few practical deployment scenarios. By the end of the book you should not only understand how to install and configure OneOps, but also be comfortable with the architecture and various components of OneOps. You will also learn advanced tasks, such as how to add new components to OneOps, how to add unsupported and custom clouds, and how to interact with OneOps using the REST API.

What this book covers

Chapter 1, *Getting Started with OneOps*, shows various ways to install OneOps as a standalone system. It shows how to use the Amazon Machine Image as well as the Vagrant Image to install your own OneOps copy as a sandbox for development, testing or even production. It will also introduce you to some key OneOps concepts.

Chapter 2, *Understanding the OneOps Architecture*, gives a detailed view of the OneOps backend architecture. It gives an overview of all the backend services, their purposes, and how they all work together. It will also introduce you to a couple of handy utilities that will enable you to look at the backend CMS data.

Chapter 3, *OneOps Application Life Cycle*, takes you on your first steps towards Application Lifecycle Management using OneOps. You will take your first steps in OneOps by creating and configuring a cloud and adding services under it. You will then design an assembly by using readymade packs provided by OneOps. You will also learn how to create environments and how to transition your assembly across the environments. Finally, you will learn how to monitor your assembly.

Chapter 4, *OneOps Enterprise Deployment*, deals with enterprise deployment of OneOps. It will show you the things you will have to consider before planning an enterprise deployment. It will also show you how to use OneOps to install an enterprise version of OneOps, which parameters to configure, how to configure backups, among other things. You will also learn more about the configuration of individual services.

Chapter 5, *Practical Deployment Scenario*, will show you a very common and practical deployment scenario and walk you through it. You will be using OneOps to deploy a load balanced website consisting of Apache HTTPD, Tomcat, and Mysql. We will build on top of this architecture to add SSL to the website. After adding SSL, we will then be adding autorepair and autoscaling and enabling the applications to be deployed to multiple clouds. We will also look at various common errors and get a feel for how to resolve them.

Chapter 6, *Managing Your OneOps*, will show you how to upgrade your OneOps installation with minimal downtime. You will learn how to upgrade OneOps both for Standalone and Enterprise installation. You will also learn how to configure database backups. This chapter will also show you how to handle and configure security groups.

Chapter 7, *Working with Functional Components*, tells you in detail about the functional components of OneOps, namely the circuit and inductor. You will find out how to build, install, and configure an inductor. You will also get an introduction to circuits and learn how to configure them.

Chapter 8, *Building Components for OneOps*, starts with a brief recap of OneOps architecture.

It will show you how OneOps can be extended by creating your own components by introducing components to you. You will also get familiar with the concepts of platforms and assemblies in this chapter.

Chapter 9, *Adding and Managing OneOps Components*, will have you create a new OneOps component step by step and add it to your OneOps instance. You will also be installing and testing the new component and updating the CMS to reflect it. You will also be creating a new platform pack. This chapter will also teach you how to maintain your components, maintain your platform packs, and add monitoring to your components.

Chapter 10, *Adding Your Own Cloud to OneOps*, teaches you to add a previously unsupported cloud to OneOps. Although OneOps comes with quite a few clouds supported out of the box, this chapter shows you how to add an unsupported cloud step by step. It will tell you all the things you need to consider when adding a custom cloud and then show you how to add a compute instance by adding support for DigitalOcean droplets. It will also show you how to add monitoring for your droplets.

Chapter 11, *Integrating with OneOps Using API*, shows how you can leverage the functionality of OneOps from other applications using the REST API. It shows you how to create and transition an assembly using easy to understand scripts written in Ruby that calls the REST API provided by OneOps.

What you need for this book

This book assumes you have basic knowledge of Linux Operating System. It also assumes you have basic knowledge of DevOps practices. This book will go from the basic setup to the advanced setup of OneOps and its related functions. All the configurations and tasks mentioned in this book will work on a basic standalone setup and have been tested as such. So, to run anything from this book you will need at least a standalone setup on your desktop, laptop, or in the cloud. The most common way to set up is, as mentioned in Chapter 1, *Getting Started with OneOps*, to install VirtualBox and then Vagrant and then follow the instructions provided by OneOps. The following hardware resources are required to run OneOps:

- CPUs: 4 cores
- Memory: 16 GB
- Disk space: 80 GB

The following software is needed to run OneOps:

- Linux Operating System: Centos 7.x
- VirtualBox
- AWS or Azure account

Internet connectivity is required to connect to, install, and manager other clouds.

Who this book is for

This book is for those who want to accelerate their deployments. This book is for those who want to get away from monolithic builds and deployments. This book is for those who want to give more control to developers while making developers responsible for their own applications in all environments. This book is for those who want more visibility in their application process across the spectrum. This book is for those who love automation. This book is for those who want to embrace DevOps, or for those who just want to take it for a drive. No prior knowledge of anything is assumed.

Conventions

In this book, you will find a number of text styles that distinguish between different kinds of information. Here are some examples of these styles and an explanation of their meaning.

Code words in text, database table names, folder names, filenames, file extensions, pathnames, dummy URLs, user input, and Twitter handles are shown as follows: "The next lines of code read the link and assign it to the to the `BeautifulSoup` function."

A block of code is set as follows:

```
monitors => {
'Log' => {:description => 'Log',
:source => '',
:chart => {'min' => 0, 'unit' => ''},
```

Any command-line input or output is written as follows:

```
$ aws ec2 create-key-pair --key-name OneOpsAuth --query
'KeyMaterial' --output 'text' > OneOpsAuth.pem
```

New terms and **important words** are shown in bold. Words that you see on the screen, for example, in menus or dialog boxes, appear in the text like this: "Select a region you want to add. Currently supported regions are **US-East-1**, **US-West-1**, and **US-West-2**"

Warnings or important notes appear in a box like this.

Tips and tricks appear like this.

Reader feedback

Feedback from our readers is always welcome. Let us know what you think about this book-what you liked or disliked. Reader feedback is important for us as it helps us develop titles that you will really get the most out of.

To send us general feedback, simply e-mail feedback@packtpub.com, and mention the book's title in the subject of your message.

If there is a topic that you have expertise in and you are interested in either writing or contributing to a book, see our author guide at www.packtpub.com/authors.

Customer support

Now that you are the proud owner of a Packt book, we have a number of things to help you to get the most from your purchase.

Downloading the example code

You can download the example code files for this book from your account at http://www.packtpub.com. If you purchased this book elsewhere, you can visit http://www.packtpub.com/support and register to have the files e-mailed directly to you.

You can download the code files by following these steps:

1. Log in or register to our website using your e-mail address and password.
2. Hover the mouse pointer on the **SUPPORT** tab at the top.
3. Click on **Code Downloads & Errata**.

4. Enter the name of the book in the **Search** box.
5. Select the book for which you're looking to download the code files.
6. Choose from the drop-down menu where you purchased this book from.
7. Click on **Code Download**.

Once the file is downloaded, please make sure that you unzip or extract the folder using the latest version of:

- WinRAR / 7-Zip for Windows
- Zipeg / iZip / UnRarX for Mac
- 7-Zip / PeaZip for Linux

The code bundle for the book is also hosted on GitHub at `https://github.com/PacktPubl ishing/Practical-OneOps`. We also have other code bundles from our rich catalog of books and videos available at `https://github.com/PacktPublishing/`. Check them out!

Downloading the color images of this book

We also provide you with a PDF file that has color images of the screenshots/diagrams used in this book. The color images will help you better understand the changes in the output. You can download this file from `https://www.packtpub.com/sites/default/files/down loads/PracticalOneOps_ColorImages.pdf`.

Errata

Although we have taken every care to ensure the accuracy of our content, mistakes do happen. If you find a mistake in one of our books-maybe a mistake in the text or the code-we would be grateful if you could report this to us. By doing so, you can save other readers from frustration and help us improve subsequent versions of this book. If you find any errata, please report them by visiting `http://www.packtpub.com/submit-errata`, selecting your book, clicking on the **Errata Submission Form** link, and entering the details of your errata. Once your errata are verified, your submission will be accepted and the errata will be uploaded to our website or added to any list of existing errata under the Errata section of that title.

To view the previously submitted errata, go to `https://www.packtpub.com/books/conten t/support` and enter the name of the book in the search field. The required information will appear under the **Errata** section.

Piracy

Piracy of copyrighted material on the Internet is an ongoing problem across all media. At Packt, we take the protection of our copyright and licenses very seriously. If you come across any illegal copies of our works in any form on the Internet, please provide us with the location address or website name immediately so that we can pursue a remedy.

Please contact us at copyright@packtpub.com with a link to the suspected pirated material.

We appreciate your help in protecting our authors and our ability to bring you valuable content.

Questions

If you have a problem with any aspect of this book, you can contact us at questions@packtpub.com, and we will do our best to address the problem.

1

Getting Started with OneOps

Since you are reading this book, you are probably keen to get up-and-running with OneOps. Deploying OneOps in an enterprise environment is a complex task. It is always prudent to start with a test installation. A test installation allows you to test all the features in isolation without affecting your current network and applications. You can also use a test installation as your developer sandbox.

A fully fledged OneOps installation consists of lot of moving parts and complex configurations. Fortunately, almost all of these are automated and for the test install they come in nice little bundles. This chapter will show you two ways to configure a test installation that can also be used as developer sandbox. We will then see how to configure our first installation of OneOps. The two ways you can install OneOps are:

- Amazon AMI
- Vagrant

Amazon AMI

There are multiple reasons why you may want to run OneOps on AWS rather than your own infrastructure. Running on AWS offloads all your infrastructure management needs to Amazon so you can focus on delivery. This is crucial for you if you want to keep your DevOps team small. If the rest of your infrastructure, services, and application are also on AWS, it makes strategic sense to have your management software on AWS too. Finally, AWS provides easy options for redundancy and scalability. The downside of this option is that you cannot add your own custom cloud that runs on your own premises without considerable configuration, for example, a VPN tunnel.

OneOps provides a basic AMI in the public marketplace on Amazon AWS. This AMI comes with some basic configuration already in place to get you up-and-running. Instantiating OneOps on AWS is the quickest way you can get up and running with OneOps. There are two ways you can do this. They are as follows:

- Using the AWS command line tool
- Using the AWS web-based console

Knowing how to spin up the OneOps AMI from the command line comes in handy as you can make it a part of your automation or DevOps delivery chain later.

 You can find more details on installing the AWS command line tool here: http://docs.aws.amazon.com/cli/latest/userguide/installing.htm l.

Once you have the command line tool installed, the first step is to generate a keypair, which you will use to connect to the new instance you will spin up.

1. Run the command following to generate the keypair.

```
$ aws ec2 create-key-pair --key-name OneOpsAuth
--query 'KeyMaterial' --output 'text' > OneOpsAuth.pem
```

2. Once the keypair is generated, create a security group to control the traffic to the instance.

```
$ aws ec2 create-security-group --group-name OneOps-sg
--description "Oneops Security Group"
{
   "GroupId": "sg-05e2847d"
}
```

Note the GroupId of the group that you just created as we will need it when we open up ports. We will now open up access to ports 22 and 3000, port 22 so you can SSH to it remotely and 3000 because the OneOps frontend is a *Ruby on Rails* application and is accessible on port 3000.

```
$ aws ec2 authorize-security-group-ingress --group-id
sg-903004f8 --protocol tcp --port 22 --cidr 0.0.0.0/0
$ aws ec2 authorize-security-group-ingress --group-id
sg-903004f8 --protocol tcp --port 3000 --cidr 0.0.0.0/0
```

Note that we opened up access to the whole world on port 22 and 3000 by giving access to 0.0.0.0/0. If you always login from a fixed set of IP addresses, such as a corporate network, you might want to secure your installation by giving access to that set of IP addresses only.

3. Finally verify that your security group was created successfully and the permissions were applied correctly.

```
$ aws ec2 describe-security-groups --group-id sg-05e2847d
{
"SecurityGroups": [
    {
        "IpPermissionsEgress": [
            {
                "IpProtocol": "-1",
                "IpRanges": [
                    {
                        "CidrIp": "0.0.0.0/0"
                    }
                ],
                "UserIdGroupPairs": [],
                "PrefixListIds": []
            }
        ],
        "Description": "OneOps Security Group",
        "IpPermissions": [
            {
                "PrefixListIds": [],
                "FromPort": 22,
                "IpRanges": [
                    {
                        "CidrIp": "0.0.0.0/0"
                    }
                ],
                "ToPort": 22,
                "IpProtocol": "tcp",
                "UserIdGroupPairs": []
            },
            {
                "PrefixListIds": [],
                "FromPort": 3000,
                "IpRanges": [
                    {
                        "CidrIp": "0.0.0.0/0"
                    }
                ],
                "ToPort": 3000,
```

```
                    "IpProtocol": "tcp",
                    "UserIdGroupPairs": []
              }
          ],
          "GroupName": "OneOps-sg",
          "VpcId": "vpc-45e3af21",
          "OwnerId": "377640004228",
          "GroupId": "sg-05e2847d"
      }
  ]
}
```

Finally, we are almost ready to launch the AMI. However, for that we need the instance ID for the correct AMI. OneOps AMI names are structured as **OneOps-basic-preconf-v*** where * is 1.1, 1.2.

4. To find the latest version of image available run the command following:

```
$ aws ec2 describe-images --filter "Name=name,Values=OneOps*"
--query 'Images[*].{Name:Name,ID:ImageId}'
[
    {
        "Name": "OneOps-basic-preconf-v1.3",
        "ID": "ami-076c416d"
    },
{
        "Name": "OneOps-basic-preconf-v1.2",
        "ID": "ami-fc1b3996"
    }
]
```

Once you have the AMI ID, you are now ready to launch the OneOps instance.

5. Run the following command to launch the AMI instance.

```
$ aws ec2 run-instances --image-id ami-076c416d
--count 1 --instance-type m4.large
--key-name OneOpsAuth --security-group-ids sg-05e2847d
{
"OwnerId": "377640004228",
"ReservationId": "r-e8a1e943",
"Instances": [
    {
        "Hypervisor": "xen",
        "PublicDnsName": "",
        "VpcId": "vpc-45e3af21",
        "RootDeviceName": "/dev/sda1",
        "StateReason": {
```

```
            "Message": "pending",
            "Code": "pending"
        },
        "ProductCodes": [],
        "ClientToken": "",
        "Architecture": "x86_64",
        "SubnetId": "subnet-2311d009",
        "State": {
            "Name": "pending",
            "Code": 0
        },
        "PrivateIpAddress": "172.31.56.32",
        "InstanceId": "i-4af1d7c9",
        "SecurityGroups": [
            {
                "GroupId": "sg-05e2847d",
                "GroupName": "OneOps-sg"
            }
        ],
        "EbsOptimized": false,
        "VirtualizationType": "hvm",
        "KeyName": "OneOpsAuth",
        "Placement": {
            "AvailabilityZone": "us-east-1b",
            "Tenancy": "default",
            "GroupName": ""
        },
        "StateTransitionReason": "",
        "ImageId": "ami-076c416d",
        "Monitoring": {
            "State": "disabled"
        },
        "SourceDestCheck": true,
        "InstanceType": "m4.large",
        "BlockDeviceMappings": [],
        "RootDeviceType": "ebs",
        "PrivateDnsName":
            "ip-172-31-56-32.ec2.internal",
        "NetworkInterfaces": [
            {
                "PrivateIpAddress": "172.31.56.32",
                "PrivateIpAddresses": [
                    {
                        "PrivateIpAddress": "172.31.56.32",
                        "Primary": true,
                        "PrivateDnsName":
                            "ip-172-31-56- 32.ec2.internal"
                    }
```

Getting Started with OneOps

```
        ],
        "MacAddress": "12:a5:58:7e:f5:f1",
        "VpcId": "vpc-45e3af21",
        "Groups": [
            {
                "GroupId": "sg-05e2847d",
                "GroupName": "OneOps-sg"
            }
        ],
        "OwnerId": "377649884228",
        "SourceDestCheck": true,
        "Attachment": {
            "DeleteOnTermination": true,
            "AttachTime": "2016-03-24T19:53:13.000Z",
            "Status": "attaching",
            "DeviceIndex": 0,
            "AttachmentId": "eni-attach-9a96416b"
        },
        "PrivateDnsName":
            "ip-172-31-56-32.ec2.internal",
        "Status": "in-use",
        "Description": "",
        "SubnetId": "subnet-2311d009",
        "NetworkInterfaceId": "eni-2aeed90f"
    }
        ],
        "LaunchTime": "2016-03-24T19:53:13.000Z",
        "AmiLaunchIndex": 0
    }
        ],
        "Groups": []
}
```

`image-id` is the ID you obtained from the previous query for the latest image version (in this case v1.3). The `key name` is the new key you created and the security group is the group you created. Replace the values in the preceding command as needed. Make sure the `InstanceType` is `m4.large` as OneOps needs at least 8 GB of memory to run. The image will also attach two block devices to the instance for storage. Give the instance a few minutes to start. Lastly tag the instance with a tag called OneOps so you can easily find it. For this you will need the `InstanceId`. For example, in the previous output, you can see the `InstanceId` for the instance created above is `i-4af1d7c9`.

That's it! Now look up the public IP of your instance and connect to it at port 3000. You should see the OneOps login screen.

```
$ aws ec2 describe-instances --filter "Name=tag:Name,Values=OneOps"
{
"Reservations": [
    {
        "Groups": [],
        "OwnerId": "377649884228",
        "ReservationId": "r-e8a1e943",
        "Instances": [
            {
                "PublicIpAddress": "54.86.6.251",
                "State": {
                    "Code": 16,
                    "Name": "running"
                },
                "Architecture": "x86_64",
                "LaunchTime": "2016-03-24T19:53:13.000Z",
                "SubnetId": "subnet-2311d009",
                "ProductCodes": [],
                "PrivateIpAddress": "172.31.56.32",
                "Monitoring": {
                    "State": "disabled"
                },
                "PrivateDnsName": "ip-172-31-56-32.ec2.internal",
                "NetworkInterfaces": [
                    {
                        "Groups": [
                            {
                                "GroupId": "sg-05e2847d",
                                "GroupName": "OneOps-sg"
                            }
                        ],
                        "OwnerId": "377649884228",
                        "NetworkInterfaceId": "eni-2aeed90f",
                        "SourceDestCheck": true,
                        "SubnetId": "subnet-2311d009",
                        "PrivateIpAddress": "172.31.56.32",
                        "Status": "in-use",
                        "MacAddress": "12:a5:58:7e:f5:f1",
                            "VpcId": "vpc-45e3af21",
                        "Description": "",
                        "PrivateDnsName":
                            "ip-172-31-56-32.ec2.internal",
                        "PrivateIpAddresses": [
                            {
                                "Association": {
```

```
                        "PublicIp": "54.86.6.251",
                        "IpOwnerId": "amazon",
                        "PublicDnsName":
                            "ec2-54-86-6-251.compute-
                            1.amazonaws.com"
                    },
                    "PrivateDnsName":
                        "ip-172-31-56-32.ec2.internal",
                    "PrivateIpAddress": "172.31.56.32",
                    "Primary": true
                }
            ],
            "Attachment": {
                "DeviceIndex": 0,
                "AttachTime": "2016-03-24T19:53:13.000Z",
                "AttachmentId": "eni-attach-9a96416b",
                "DeleteOnTermination": true,
                    "Status": "attached"
            },
            "Association": {
                "PublicIp": "54.86.6.251",
                "IpOwnerId": "amazon",
                "PublicDnsName":
                    "ec2-54-86-6-251.compute-
                    1.amazonaws.com"
            }
        }
    ],
    "ImageId": "ami-076c416d",
    "RootDeviceType": "ebs",
    "KeyName": "OneOpsAuth",
    "Placement": {
        "AvailabilityZone": "us-east-1b",
        "Tenancy": "default",
        "GroupName": ""
    },
    "Hypervisor": "xen",
    "RootDeviceName": "/dev/sda1",
    "Tags": [
        {
            "Key": "Name",
            "Value": "OneOps"
        }
    ],
    "VirtualizationType": "hvm",
    "SourceDestCheck": true,
    "VpcId": "vpc-45e3af21",
    "StateTransitionReason": "",
```

```
        "ClientToken": "",
        "AmiLaunchIndex": 0,
        "InstanceType": "m4.large",
        "EbsOptimized": false,
        "InstanceId": "i-4af1d7c9",
        "BlockDeviceMappings": [
            {
                "DeviceName": "/dev/sda1",
                "Ebs": {
                    "AttachTime": "2016-03-24T19:53:14.000Z",
                    "DeleteOnTermination": false,
                    "VolumeId": "vol-a0c6837e",
                    "Status": "attached"
                }
            },
            {
                "DeviceName": "/dev/sdb",
                "Ebs": {
                    "AttachTime": "2016-03-24T19:53:14.000Z",
                    "DeleteOnTermination": false,
                    "VolumeId": "vol-23c782fd",
                    "Status": "attached"
                }
            }
        ],
        "SecurityGroups": [
            {
                "GroupId": "sg-05e2847d",
                "GroupName": "OneOps-sg"
            }
        ],
        "PublicDnsName":
            "ec2-54-86-6-251.compute-1.amazonaws.com"
      }
    ]
  }
 ]
}
```

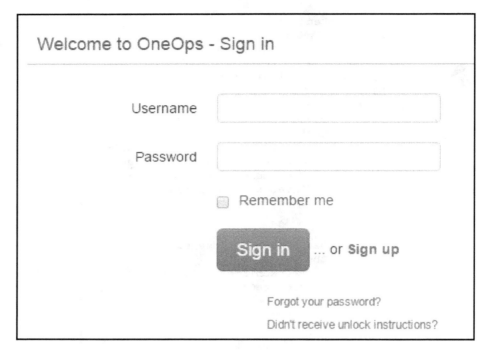

Although it's nice to know how to create a OneOps instance from the command line and it does come in handy if you want to make it part of your automation, the same results can be obtained in a much quicker way through the Amazon AWS console.

On the AWS console:

1. Select **EC2**.
2. Then select **Instances** from the left navigation bar.
3. Click the big blue **Launch Instance** button on the top.
4. On the left navigation bar click on **Community AMIs**.
5. Search for **OneOps**.

You may see several results for OneOps AMIs as shown in the following screenshot:

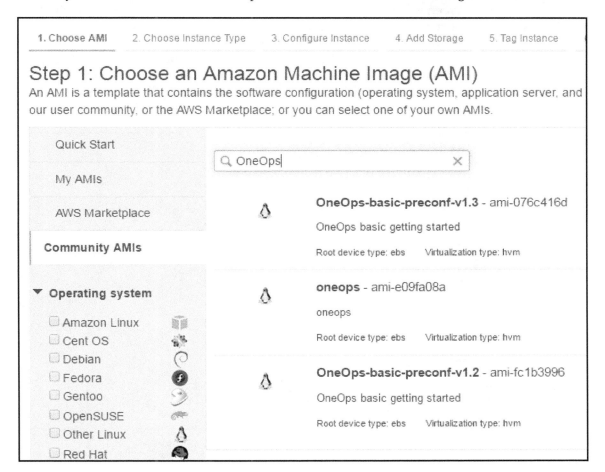

Select the AMI with the latest revision number; in the screenshot preceding it is v1.3. Click **Select**. On the next screen you will be asked what kind of instance you want to launch. If you have the one-year free membership from Amazon, it is very tempting to launch the **t2.micro** instance, which is eligible for the free tier. However OneOps will give very poor performance on micro instances and may even fail to launch fully due to a lack of resources. To perform well OneOps needs at least 8 GB of memory. It is recommended you use at least the **m4.large** instance, which comes with 2 vCPUs and 8 GB of memory. Select **m4.large** and click on **Next** which will allow you to configure and review instance details.

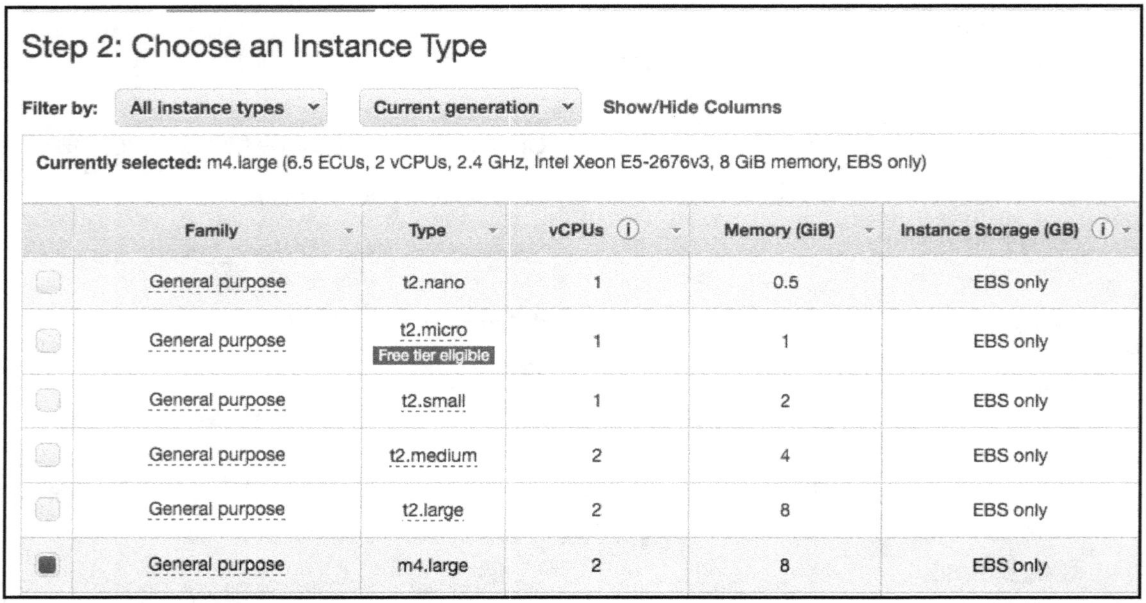

Step 2: Choose an Instance Type

Filter by: **All instance types** ∨   **Current generation** ∨   Show/Hide Columns

Currently selected: m4.large (6.5 ECUs, 2 vCPUs, 2.4 GHz, Intel Xeon E5-2676v3, 8 GiB memory, EBS only)

	Family	Type	vCPUs ⓘ	Memory (GiB)	Instance Storage (GB) ⓘ
○	General purpose	t2.nano	1	0.5	EBS only
○	General purpose	t2.micro Free tier eligible	1	1	EBS only
○	General purpose	t2.small	1	2	EBS only
○	General purpose	t2.medium	2	4	EBS only
○	General purpose	t2.large	2	8	EBS only
●	General purpose	m4.large	2	8	EBS only

On this screen a few options are of interest. Keep the number of instances to **1**. Don't request a spot instance as they are best used for batch jobs and processes that are fault-tolerant. Select the defaults for the rest. Make sure you assign a public IP if you want your OneOps instance to be accessible from the outside world. You can also add protection against accidental termination and **CloudWatch** monitoring from here. Amazon charges extra for CloudWatch monitoring; however, if you will be using OneOps for a long period and ultimately carrying it over into production, you should select **CloudWatch**. Lastly the `Tenancy` of the instance will also affect its performance. For most purposes a shared instance should be fine.

Step 3: Configure Instance Details

Configure the instance to suit your requirements. You can launch multiple instances from the same AMI, request Spot instances to take advantage of the lower pricing, assign an access management role to the instance, and more.

Number of instances ⓘ	1 Launch into Auto Scaling Group ⓘ
Purchasing option ⓘ	☐ Request Spot instances
Network ⓘ	vpc-45e3af21 (172.31.0.0/16) (default) C Create new VPC
Subnet ⓘ	No preference (default subnet in any Availability Zone) Create new subnet
Auto-assign Public IP ⓘ	Use subnet setting (Enable)
Placement group ⓘ	No placement group
IAM role ⓘ	None C Create new IAM role
Shutdown behavior ⓘ	Stop
Enable termination protection ⓘ	☐ Protect against accidental termination
Monitoring ⓘ	☐ Enable CloudWatch detailed monitoring Additional charges apply.

Click on **Next** to review the storage. The AMI already comes with two volumes attached to it: a root volume of 10 GB and an additional volume of 40 GB. You can increase the size of the additional volume as most of OneOps is stored in `/opt/oneops`. You can also select the **Delete on Termination** options if you are just trying out OneOps since the storage volumes will not be terminated on instance termination and Amazon will charge you for volume storage. After making your changes, click **Next** to tag your instance. Here you can create tags as name/value pairs. Create a tag with the name **Name** and the value as **OneOps** to easily identify your instance. Click **Next** to configure the security group. Create a new group called **OneOps-sg**. Make sure port `22` is enabled so you can SSH to your instance. Also enable access to port `3000`; OneOps is a *Ruby on Rails* application and binds to port `3000`.

It is not really prudent to open access to all IP addresses and Amazon will warn you against that. If you know the range of IP addresses you will be logging in from, restrict access to that range.

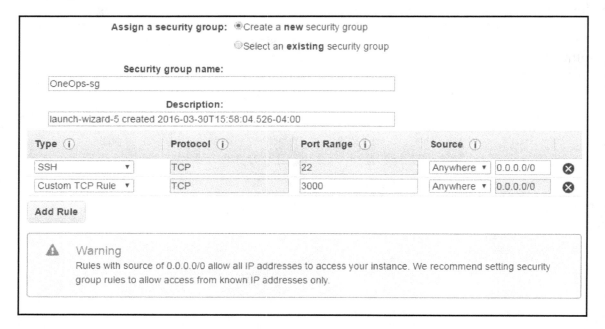

You are now ready to review and launch your instance. You may get a couple of warnings. If you are on the free tier, you will get a warning that this instance is not eligible for the free tier since you selected **m4.large**. You will also get a warning that access to your instance is open to the world. Review the warnings and click **Launch**. Once you click **Launch**, you will be asked to either create a new keypair or use an existing keypair to attach to the instance. If you have an existing keypair that you have access to, select it here or else generate a new keypair and download the key. Be warned if you lose this key, you will be unable to SSH to the instance to keep this key in a safe place. Click on **Launch** instance. The instance will take some time to initialize. OneOps will also take some time to initialize. Once the initialization is done, you can connect to port 3000 via a browser and you should see a login screen as shown in the image above. You can also use the key you generated to login to the instance to have a look around. Make sure to use **centos** as the username. You can SSH to your instance directly from a compatible browser as shown in the following screenshot.

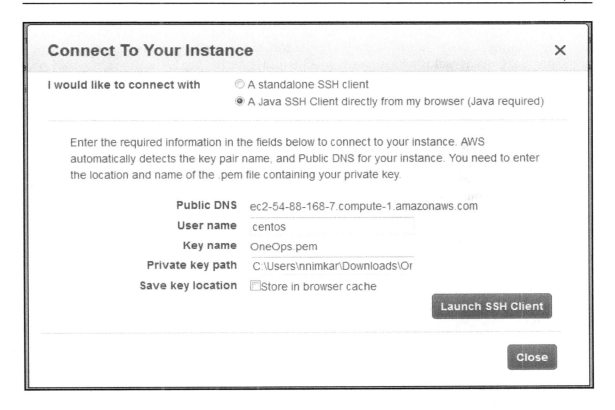

Vagrant

You can also launch a copy of OneOps using **Vagrant**. Vagrant is a orchestration tool from HashiCorp used to create lightweight and portable development environments. This is particularly useful if you want to create a OneOps installation on a laptop that you will carry with you. You can also create your own OneOps development environment using Vagrant.

 Download the latest version of VirtualBox from the Oracle VirtualBox website (`https://www.virtualbox.org/wiki/Downloads`) and install it. Also download and install the latest version of Vagrant from the Vagrant website (`https://www.vagrantup.com/downloads.html`).

Also install the extension packages for VirtualBox. These install instructions will work on the Mac or Linux. Currently the Vagrant installation does not work on Windows. Go ahead and clone the OneOps setup repository from GitHub:

```
git clone https://github.com/oneops/setup
cd setup/vagrant-centos7
```

Before you start the Vagrant install, you can tune your installation to allocate more resources to your OneOps install. By default, your OneOps install will have only 1 CPU and 8 GB memory. If the host machine has more resources available, it is recommended you allocate more resources to your VM too. This will increase the performance of your OneOps installation.

Open `Vagrantfile` and find the `vb.memory` line. It will be set to 8 GB. Increase it to about half the size of your host operating system. Below that, add the line `vb.cpus` and give it a value of about half the number of CPUs available to your host machine. Make sure you tune it this way only if nothing else is running on the host machine. Reduce the allocation if you have other things running too. You are now ready to run `vagrant up`. Vagrant up starts to build OneOps for you. It does so by executing the following steps.

1. Vagrant imports CentOS box and creates a centos virtual machine to build a OneOps installation on top of.
2. It runs `oneops-jreqs.sh`, which installs java, postgres, vim and git among other things.
3. It runs `install-es.sh`, which installs `elasticsearch`.
4. It runs `install-rvm.sh`, which installs the current stable version of Ruby.
5. It runs `install-ruby.sh`, which installs *Ruby on Rails* and other modules required to run the OneOps frontend
6. It runs `install-logstash.sh`, which installs and configures `logstash`.
7. Finally it runs `oo-setup.sh`, which clones the `dev-tools` repository and runs all the scripts in the setup-scripts directory to actually set up OneOps.

After the installation is done you will see a message like the following.

```
nnimkar@nnimkar1: ~/scripts/vagrant/oneops/vagrant
==> default:         exist   clouds-enabled/shared
==> default:         success Next Step: inductor start ; inductor tail
==> default:         start   public_ip consumer
==> default: pgrep: invalid option -- 'a'
==> default: Usage: pgrep [-flvx] [-d DELIM]
==> default: [-n|-o] [-P PPIDLIST] [-g PGRPLIST] [-s SIDLIST]
==> default:     [-u EUIDLIST] [-U UIDLIST] [-G GIDLIST] [-t TERMLIST] [PATTERN]
==> default:         start   public_ip logstash agent
==> default:         start   already running
==> default: pgrep: invalid option -- 'a'
==> default: Usage: pgrep [-flvx] [-d DELIM]
==> default: [-n|-o] [-P PPIDLIST] [-g PGRPLIST] [-s SIDLIST]
==> default:     [-u EUIDLIST] [-U UIDLIST] [-G GIDLIST] [-t TERMLIST] [PATTERN]
==> default:         start   shared logstash agent
==> default:         running cp -f /usr/local/rvm/gems/ruby-1.9.3-p551/gems/oneops
-admin-1.0.0/lib/templates/inductor/init.d/inductor /etc/init.d/inductor
==> default: done with inductor
==> default: Starting display
==> default: [  OK  ]
==> default: OneOps should be up on http://localhost:3000
==> default: Configure your port forwarding and shut down iptables service (or c
onfigure it) if needed
==> default: All done at : 20:28:29
nnimkar@nnimkar1:~/scripts/vagrant/oneops/vagrant$
```

However, in a vagrant install, the port actually gets mapped on port 9090 of the host OS. So, if you want to try your new OneOps installation, you should connect to http://localhost:9090.

OneOps application key concepts

OneOps is a complex application that facilitates DevOps. As such it uses its own terminology and introduces its own concepts. Once you familiarize yourself with these concepts you are one step closer to understanding OneOps.

Organization

An **organization** in OneOps is a group under which various teams, clouds, assemblies, and services can be logically grouped. An organization can be your whole organization, a sub-unit of the organization, a single group inside the organization or any combination of those. You can create organizations to logically organize your projects, sub-projects, applications of all sizes.. In that respect organizations can also be various projects in your organizations. It is entirely up to you how you define an organization.

User

A **user** is a single user with a single login to whom you can assign permissions and responsibilities inside of OneOps. You can group various users into a team.

Team

You can group various users into **teams**. You can logically group several users into cohesive teams to make management of your users simple. This also simplifies permissions. You can assign permissions to the whole team instead of individual users, for example, the development team, QA team, operations team, DevOps team, and so on.

Clouds

Clouds are groups of common services that are offered under a common tag. By themselves clouds are nothing but a label and are not functional at all. They just act as an aggregator under which you can group various public (AWS compute, Azure compute, AWS DNS, and so on) or private (OpenStack) services. It is a good idea to give a descriptive name to the cloud. For example, if you are creating a cloud to group together some AWS services such as AWS EC2, Route 53 DNS, and S3 DNS, then it's a good idea to call it AmazonCloud instead of MyCloud.

Services

As mentioned above, a cloud is just a tag and is of little use until you add a **service** to it. You can add a public service to it, provided you have a key, such as AWS EC2, or you can add a private service to it such as Nova Compute from OpenStack (if you have your own OpenStack installation).

Assembly

An **assembly**, as defined by OneOps, is the definition of an application architecture and all its components including its infrastructure. OneOps provides a very visual way of defining an assembly. Assemblies are highly customizable and portable; once defined, they can be deployed to any target cloud without any more changes. Assemblies are defined by adding different platforms to them and defining relationships between them.

Platforms

Platforms as prepackaged software templates that can be installed from packs. Some examples of platforms are MySQL, HAProxy, and so on. OneOps comes with a robust pack preinstalled. You can also define your own pack or add to the existing pack by following the template.

Summary

In this chapter we learned how to do a test installation of OneOps on Amazon Web Services. We saw two handy methods to do so, one from command line, which is useful for automation, and the second from the console, which quickly achieves the same results. We also explored how to do a test installation using Vagrant and Docker. Finally, we saw how to create a user and an organization. We also saw some key concepts of OneOps.

In the next chapter we will dig a little deeper into the OneOps architecture to see what makes it tick. We will take a close look at various backend components as well as the OneOps command line. We will also look at OneOps concepts such as inductor, antenna, work order, and action order.

2
Understanding the OneOps Architecture

In the previous chapter, you learned how to do a test installation of OneOps, which you can use as a developer sandbox or a proof of concept. For a more permanent installation, it is important to understand the architecture of OneOps. In this chapter, we will take a look at the OneOps architecture, its various components, their purposes, and how they interact with each other.

The OneOps team defines OneOps as a multi-cloud application orchestrator that lets you design your application in a cloud-agnostic way. OneOps abstracts away multiple cloud providers and manages applications, design, deployments, operations, and monitoring.

The OneOps system architecture

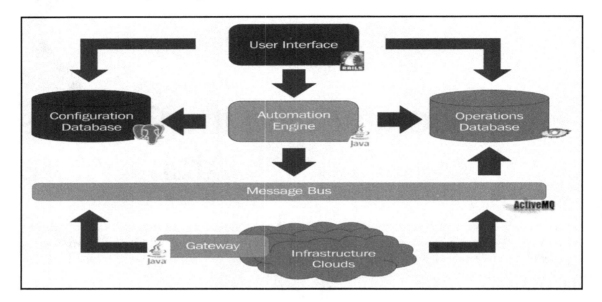

The OneOps system architecture

OneOps uses a web frontend written in Ruby on Rails to provide a self-service portal to users, as well as access to REST APIs to automate several tasks. It also has a middleware automation engine and a backend that stores data in several databases based on different needs. These broad components are further broken down into smaller components that connect and communicate with each other, either via databases or a message bus.

OneOps uses several technologies behind the scenes to create an ecosystem of services and applications.

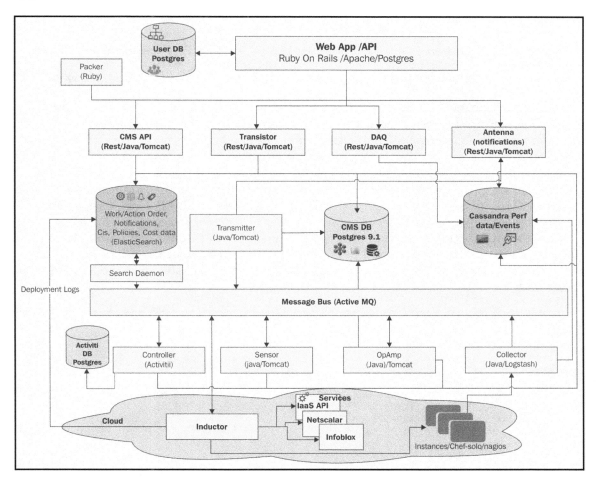

OneOps detailed system architecture

Display

OneOps provides a web-based self-service portal written in Ruby on Rails named **Display**. Because Display is a OneOps's window to the world and is written in Rails, pretty much all aspects of it are customizable.

If you are trying to install and run Display by itself on a Mac OS X machine, you will have to run the following command, as the dynamic linked `postgres` library has to be explicitly provided to the `pg gem`:

```
pg gem install issue on osx: gem install pg -v 0.17.0 -- --with-pg-
config=/Library/PostgreSQL/9.1/bin/pg_config
export DYLD_LIBRARY_PATH=/library/PostgreSQL/9.1/lib:$DYLD_LIBRARY_PATH
```

Once Display is installed, you can find settings in the `/opt/oneops/config` directory. Most of the settings can be set in two ways. You can either set the corresponding environment variable or change the setting file in the `config` directory. The environment variables always override the configuration set in the file. You can customize everything, starting with the logo, system name (default is OneOps), support e-mail, news URL, help URL, feedback URL, and URLs for terms of service and privacy policy. You can also configure OneOps to authenticate, either against a database or LDAP. OneOps also has support for OmniAuth, which means if you sign up for developer accounts on GitHub, Twitter, LinkedIn, and Google and plug in the keys and secrets to the configuration file, then users can use their user ID and password from these sites instead of creating a brand new one. All of these settings can be found in `settings.yml`, as shown in the following screenshot:

```
# app/config/settings.yml

defaults: &defaults
  # Brand
  brand:
    image: logo-notext-32x32.png
    name: '<font color="#333333">One</font><font color="#888888">Ops</font>'
  identity: <%= ENV['IDENTITY'] || '' %>
  support_email: <%= ENV['SUPPORT_EMAIL'] %>
  news_url: <%= ENV['NEWS_URL'] %>
  help_url: <%= ENV['HELP_URL'] %>
  feedback_url: <%= ENV['FEEDBACK_URL'] || 'https://oneops.slack.com/messages/feedback/'
%>
  report_problem_url: <%= ENV['REPORT_PROBLEM_URL'] %>
  support_chat_url: <%= ENV['SUPPORT_CHAT_URL'] || 'https://oneops.slack.com/messages/hel
p/' %>
  terms_of_service_url: <%= ENV['TERMS_OF_SERVICE_URL'] %>
  privacy_policy_url: <%= ENV['PRIVACY_POLICY_URL'] %>

  # Authentication types currently supported are database|ldap
  authentication: database

  # Omniauth configuration
"settings.yml" [readonly] 124L, 4429C
```

You can consider changing the following settings in your installation:

- `image`: Upload an image or the logo of your organization and provide the name of the image file here. Make sure that it's under `/opt/oneops/app/assets/images` and is 32x32 pixels big.
- `name`: The name of your organization. The `font color` and styling can be configured here.
- `support_email`: If you have a central support e-mail ID, you can configure it here.
- `help_url`: If you have a centralized wiki or a knowledge base, provide a link to it here. It will be displayed at the bottom of every page.
- `support_chat_url`: If your support is available via chat, such as Slack or IRC, provide a link for it here, and it will be displayed on the left-hand side navigation bar.
- `terms_of_services`: If you have any terms of service, you can provide them here. They are displayed once when a user signs up. This is also a good place to display any one-time instructions to users, or SLA instructions.
- `Privacy_policy`: If you have a well-defined privacy policy, you can configure the link here and it will be displayed to the user when they log in.

You can also change settings such that anyone is allowed to register for OneOps or users can register only if they have an invitation. By default, anyone can register. You can also make users click on a confirmation link which they will receive in their e-mail before they can log in to OneOps. By default, that requirement is not enforced.

You can also choose to authenticate against an active directory instead of a database. You can configure an active directory in `ldap.yml`. We have the following code:

```
development:
  host: <%= ENV['LDAP_HOST'] || 'localhost' %>
  port: 389
  attribute: <%= ENV['LDAP_ATTRIBUTE'] || 'uid' %>
  base: <%= ENV['LDAP_BASE'] || 'ou=People,dc=com' %>
  admin_user: cn=Manager,dc=oneops,dc=com
  admin_password: admin_password
  ssl: false
  # <<: *AUTHORIZATIONS

shared:
  host: <%= ENV['LDAP_HOST'] || 'honts0101.homeoffice.wal-mart.com' %>
  port: <%= ENV['LDAP_PORT'] || '3269' %>
  attribute: <%= ENV['LDAP_ATTRIBUTE'] || 'sAMAccountName' %>
  base: <%= ENV['LDAP_BASE'] || 'dc=wal-mart,dc=com' %>
  admin_user: <%= ENV['LDAP_ADMIN_USER'] || 'cn=admin,dc=test,dc=com' %>
  admin_password: <%= ENV['LDAP_ADMIN_PASSWORD'] || 'admin_password' %>
  ssl: simple_tls
  # <<: *AUTHORIZATIONS

production:
  host: localhost
  port: 636
```

A typical ldap.yml

The active directory configuration can be provided by the Windows Enterprise team specific to your organization's domain. This way, all or some of your users, depending on your configuration, can log in to your installation without having to create a new account, simply by using their Windows username and password.

Backend databases

OneOps has three main backend data stores, all in Postgres database. During installation, OneOps creates three databases named `activitidb`, `kloopzapp`, and `kloopzdb`, along with the corresponding roles. The `activitidb` database stores all the information related to current activities happening in OneOps. The `kloopszpp` database stores all the metadata about the app, including user login names, organizations, groups, user preferences, and so on. `Kloopzdb` is the main change management database and acts as the CMDB for OneOps.

In this database, you will find all the information about the change items, change attributes, the relationships between them, change management logs, current change item states, and other change-related information. If you are familiar with change management, CMDB, and ITIL, you can browse this database directly to find more information on your change items. OneOps also fires up an instance of **Logstash** to collect all the logs generated by OneOps itself, as well as all the CI that it deploys, in a centralized place. It uses collectors to channel all the logs to Logstash.

```
kloopzcm | cm_ci                          | table | kloopzcm
kloopzcm | cm_ci_attribute_log            | table | kloopzcm
kloopzcm | cm_ci_attribute_log_2012       | table | kloopzcm
kloopzcm | cm_ci_attribute_log_2013       | table | kloopzcm
kloopzcm | cm_ci_attribute_log_2014       | table | kloopzcm
kloopzcm | cm_ci_attribute_log_2015       | table | kloopzcm
kloopzcm | cm_ci_attribute_log_2016       | table | kloopzcm
kloopzcm | cm_ci_attributes               | table | kloopzcm
kloopzcm | cm_ci_log                      | table | kloopzcm
kloopzcm | cm_ci_log_2012                 | table | kloopzcm
kloopzcm | cm_ci_log_2013                 | table | kloopzcm
kloopzcm | cm_ci_log_2014                 | table | kloopzcm
kloopzcm | cm_ci_log_2015                 | table | kloopzcm
kloopzcm | cm_ci_log_2016                 | table | kloopzcm
kloopzcm | cm_ci_relation_attr_log        | table | kloopzcm
kloopzcm | cm_ci_relation_attr_log_2012   | table | kloopzcm
kloopzcm | cm_ci_relation_attr_log_2013   | table | kloopzcm
kloopzcm | cm_ci_relation_attr_log_2014   | table | kloopzcm
kloopzcm | cm_ci_relation_attr_log_2015   | table | kloopzcm
kloopzcm | cm_ci_relation_attr_log_2016   | table | kloopzcm
kloopzcm | cm_ci_relation_attributes      | table | kloopzcm
kloopzcm | cm_ci_relation_log             | table | kloopzcm
kloopzcm | cm_ci_relation_log_2012        | table | kloopzcm
--More--
```

Besides these databases, OneOps has a few other data stores that it uses to store miscellaneous but important data. OneOps uses **Elastic Search** to store all the events generated by CMS, controller events such as work/action orders, and notifications. This helps OneOps to implement policies, generate costs, and maintain deployment/release history. OneOps also persists the health data about all its CI in a Cassandra database. It can then use these events to support functionality such as **autorepair** and **autoscale**.

Backend services

OneOps runs several backend services, each with a unique function. Running in conjunction, these services provide the actual functionality of OneOps. All the services are tied together by a messaging queue in the form of **ActiveMQ**. All services use either a dedicated or a shared queue to communicate with each other using Apache ActiveMQ.

Adapter

Adapter is a web application that runs under Tomcat and is available under port 8080. This application runs on whichever server Tomcat is installed on which is usually the same machine on which all of OneOps is installed. Adapter provides a set of RESTful APIs for **CRUD** (short for **create**, **read**, **update**, and **delete**) operations on model, change items, deployments, and namespaces. The API provided by adapter is primarily consumed by Display.

Transistor

Transistor also runs as a web application under Tomcat and is available under port 8080. The transistor service is responsible for creating design and deployment plans and comparing what is currently deployed versus what has been designed by the user. The service also ensures that what is defined for deployment conforms to the pack design.

Data acquisition

Data acquisition (**DAQ**) is responsible for capturing data via collectors, which is then used to graph monitor details in Display. DAQ integrates with Logstash to collect all the logging data. DAQ collects all KPIs via Logstash and inserts them into Cassandra. It also publishes them into ActiveMQ queues for consumption by Display as needed.

Antenna

Antenna is also a web application/API available under Tomcat. It is used internally by the opamp and controller to send notifications about deployments and unhealthy events to configured notification sinks.

 A notification sink is nothing but a receiver that will capture a message and may choose to do something with the message. Often, the receiver will just display or log the message. Currently, OneOps comes with hooks for Jabber, HTTP, and Log4j.

Transmitter

Transmitter tracks changes to the **change management system** and publishes them as events to ActiveMQ. These events can then be picked up by the other systems to be actioned upon.

You can quickly check the status of your transmitter by connecting to `http://youroneopsinstance:8080/transmitter`. This will show you whether your transmitter is running, your queue backlog, your CI events queue backlog, and the date and time of your transmitter's last run.

Controller

Controller is the main workhorse of OneOps doing the majority of the work once the button for deployment is pushed. It is an Activiti-based workflow engine responsible for processing work orders and action orders. **Activiti** is an open source business process management software available under Apache License. The Controller also runs as a web application under Tomcat and is available under port `8080`.

Collector

Collectors are part of DAQ and collect metrics from managed instances, which they then channel to Logstash. As part of the collector framework, OneOps installs a small binary on all the VMs deployed and managed by OneOps, named Logstash-Forwarder. Logstash-Forwarder, written in Go, has a very small footprint and securely transmits all the logs from the VM using the lumberjack protocol to Collector, via a HAProxy setup. Collectors, in turn, aggregate all the logs and forward them to Logstash, where they get filtered and, ultimately, get stored in Cassandra.

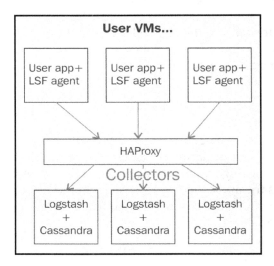

Sensor

Sensor consumes metrics that are collected by collection and analyzes them against any thresholds that have been set against all the change items. If any threshold is reached, then sensor will generate an Ops event that can be actioned upon. Sensor is based on Esper open source technology by EsperTech, which is a complex event processing and event series analysis technology. Sensor uses Espers' API to detect events in the logs and data gathered by collectors.

Opamp

The **opamp** component process Ops events generated by the sensor, specifically, events generated by unhealthy CIs. The opamp process can consume such events and generate actions to compensate for them to make the CIs healthy again. Such actions can be autorepair, autoreplace, scale-up, scale-down, and so on. Opamp reacts to such events according to the rules set in each assembly.

Inductor

The **inductor** runs as a service in the background and consumes all the work orders and action orders generated by OneOps, actions them according to their priority, and posts the results back to the controller. The inductor is responsible for executing all the steps mentioned in an assembly. An inductor is configured to listen to a cloud-specific queue through the command-line tool available via the inductor gem. The same tool also posts the results from various clouds back to the controller queue. Inductor currently supports Chef cookbooks to run various commands, but is easily extensible to support other Infrastructure as Code tools, such as Ansible, Puppet, and so on.

WorkOrder

WorkOrder is RFC or Request For Change that will result in a physical change in a CI. This typically results in an addition, updating or deletion of component in OneOps. WorkOrders are sent by controllers to message queues. Once sent, an inductor then consumes a WorkOrder and executes the associated recipe using chef-solo using the data available in the WorkOrder. Once executed, the controller then posts the response from the WorkOrder back to the queue and updates the CMS.

ActionOrder

ActionOrder is similar to WorkOrder in all aspects, except it does not result in any physical alterations of CI. As such, ActionOrder consists of actions, such as start, stop, status, repair, reboot, snapshot, restore, and so on. You may think that repair might physically alter CI, but all it does is restore CI to its previous state, so it does not count as a physical alteration.

 ITILv3 defines a CI or configuration item as any component that needs to be managed to provide an IT service. In the context of OneOps, this includes compute instances, networking infrastructure, software components, and so on.

Useful backend tools

OneOps comes with some very useful tools that allow you to navigate your way through the backend, irrespective of whether you are troubleshooting a problem or learning OneOps.

Cms-admin

Cms-admin is installed as part of OneOps and is very handy, especially if you plan to extend OneOps. Cms-admin is installed as a web app under Tomcat and is available on port 8080 on the machine where Apache Tomcat is installed. If your OneOps is installed on a server named OneOps and the Tomcat installation is on the same machine, then you can access cms-admin at http://oneops:8080/cms-admin/.

 If you are using OneOps from an Amazon EC2 install, you will have to edit Security Group and enable the port 8080 to connect to cms-admin. Again, be careful and avoid opening up access to the whole world, as there is no authentication asked for to connect to this port.

Cms-admin, at the time of writing, provides four useful tools. It provides an easy way to browse all the CMS classes provided by OneOps. This goes above and beyond the documentation available on OneOps site and will be of great interest to Java developers who are interested in extending the core OneOps functionality via Java programming. Although it does not follow the Javadoc format, it does come very close to it and gives valuable information on classes, such as name, access level, description, attributes, data types, inherited from, default values, and from and to relationship with other classes.

The second very useful tool provided by cms-admin is the CI list. It's the second link from the top and allows you to browse a lot of things configured in OneOps without actually logging on to the server. We have the following screenshot:

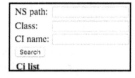

Basic search interface to CMS

This simple tool allows you to browse a lot of backend data from OneOps. For example, if you enter the namespace path as / and press *Enter*, you will see all the organizations that you configured.

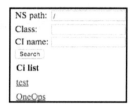

Clicking on a particular organization will show you the details of that particular organization, as shown in the following figure:

CI Detail

OneOps

Class Name :	account.Organization
Implementation:	oo::chef-11.4.0
NS Path:	/
State:	default
Comments:	
Created:	Fri Dec 18 20:32:57 UTC 2015

Attributes	DF Value	DJ Value	Comments	Owner	Created	Updated
owner	admin@oneops.com	admin@oneops.com			Fri Dec 18 20:32:57 UTC 2015	Fri Dec 18 20:32:57 UTC 2015
full_name	OneOps group	OneOps group			Fri Dec 18 20:33:34 UTC 2015	Fri Dec 18 20:33:34 UTC 2015
description					Fri Dec 18 20:33:34 UTC 2015	Fri Dec 18 20:33:34 UTC 2015

From relations:
OneOps --> base.Manages -->SimpleApache

To relations:

Entering a namespace path of `/public/oneops/packs` will show you all the built-in packs that OneOps supplies, as shown in the following screenshot:

Think of packs as ready-made, prepackaged software that OneOps provides which is ready to install on any server.

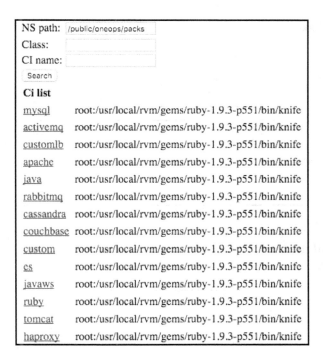

Again, clicking on a particular pack name will give you details of that pack, such as the owner, the pack type, description, and category, as shown in the upcoming figure:

CI Detail

glusterfs

Class Name :	mgmt.Pack
Implementation:	oo::chef-11.4.0
NS Path:	/public/oneops/packs
State:	default
Comments:	root:/usr/local/rvm/gems/ruby-1.9.3-p551/bin/knife
Created:	Thu Dec 17 18:29:52 UTC 2015

Attributes	DF Value	DJ Value	Comments	Owner	Created	Updated
owner					Thu Dec 17 18:29:52 UTC 2015	Thu Dec 17 18:29:52 UTC 2015
pack_type	Platform	Platform			Thu Dec 17 18:29:52 UTC 2015	Thu Dec 17 18:29:52 UTC 2015
description	GlusterFS	GlusterFS			Thu Dec 17 18:29:52 UTC 2015	Thu Dec 17 18:29:52 UTC 2015
category	Distributed Filesystems	Distributed Filesystems			Thu Dec 17 18:29:52 UTC 2015	Thu Dec 17 18:29:52 UTC 2015

From relations:

To relations:

Similarly, if you provide `/public/oneops/clouds` as the namespace path, the cms-admin tool will show you all the currently available clouds under OneOps, as shown in the following screenshot:

And, similar to the previous examples, clicking on any of the clouds will provide descriptive details on that particular cloud, as shown in the following screenshot:

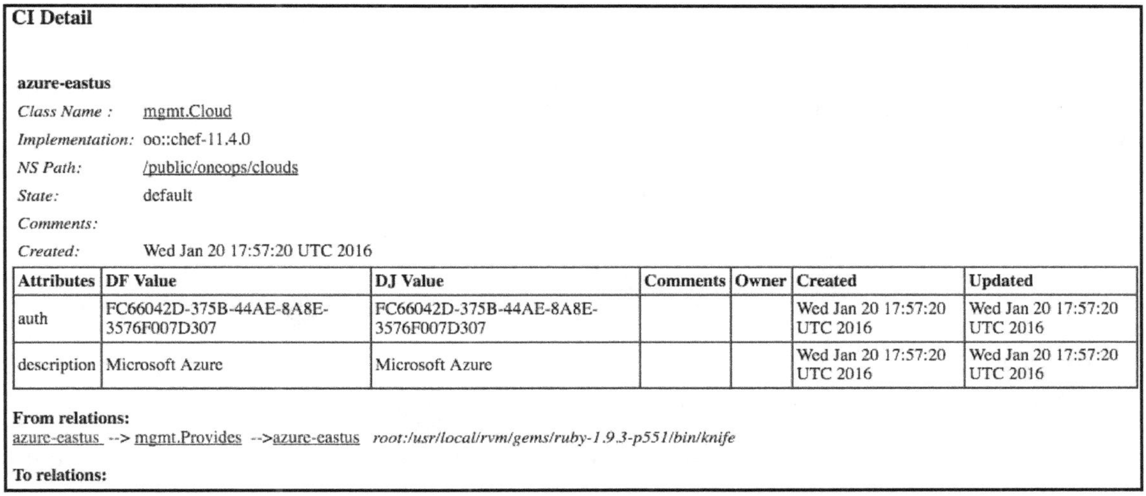

CI Detail

azure-eastus

Class Name :	mgmt.Cloud
Implementation:	oo::chef-11.4.0
NS Path:	/public/oneops/clouds
State:	default
Comments:	
Created:	Wed Jan 20 17:57:20 UTC 2016

Attributes	DF Value	DJ Value	Comments	Owner	Created	Updated
auth	FC66042D-375B-44AE-8A8E-3576F007D307	FC66042D-375B-44AE-8A8E-3576F007D307			Wed Jan 20 17:57:20 UTC 2016	Wed Jan 20 17:57:20 UTC 2016
description	Microsoft Azure	Microsoft Azure			Wed Jan 20 17:57:20 UTC 2016	Wed Jan 20 17:57:20 UTC 2016

From relations:
azure-eastus --> mgmt.Provides -->azure-eastus   *root:/usr/local/rvm/gems/ruby-1.9.3-p551/bin/knife*

To relations:

Besides the CI browser, cms-admin provides two more tools. The first is the Activiti monitor. The Activiti monitor shows all the tasks that are either in progress or have been finished by the **Activiti Business Processes Manager** that runs in the backend of OneOps, as described earlier. It provides details on the task that are in progress such as activity ID and start time. For finished tasks, it shows start time, end time, and duration. The final tool it offers is a report of stuck deployments. The stuck deployment report groups deployments under three categories:

- CMS stuck deployments
- In progress stuck deployments
- Paused stuck deployments

This is a handy way for a system administrator to get a system-wide view of deployments that are not progressing.

OneOps CLI

The OneOps command-line interface allows you to control OneOps from the command line and do everything that you can do from the GUI from the command line. This comes in very handy if you want to script a lot of tasks from OneOps but don't want to make use of the REST interface provided by OneOps. The OneOps CLI does not come installed by default. You will have to download and install it manually. You can clone it from the OneOps git repository and install it, as follows:

```
$ git clone https://github.com/oneops/cli.git
$ gem build oneops.gemspec
$ gem install oneops
```

 If you want to install the gem universally, run the last two commands as root or with sudo privileges.

Once the gem is installed, it is available as the command oneops. You can then configure it to run as follows:

```
$ oneops config set site=http://localhost:9090 -g
```

This is assuming that you installed the oneops gem on the same box as OneOps. Also, if you are running OneOps on AWS, then you should change the port to 3000. You can then log in to the site from the command line. To log in, you will need to obtain the API key. You can obtain the key from the OneOps GUI. Log in to the OneOps GUI and click on the **username** on the lower left-hand side. Then, click on the **authentication** tab. You should see the **API token** on the right-hand side of the screen, as follows:

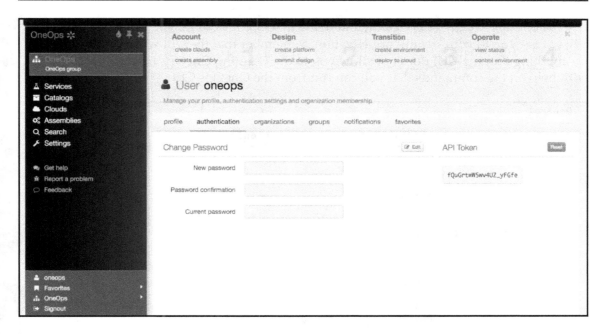

Once you obtain the API token, you can specify that as your login name with the OneOps CLI. Your password is your regular password. We have the following screenshot:

```
[root@ip-172-31-57-184 ~]# oneops auth login
Enter your OneOps credentials.
Username: fQuGrtwWSwv4UZ_yFGfe
Password (typing will be hidden):
Logged In
[root@ip-172-31-57-184 ~]# oneops config set organization=OneOps -g
[root@ip-172-31-57-184 ~]# oneops organization
{"ciId":57129,"ciName":"OneOps","ciClassName":"account.Organization","impl":"oo::chef-11.
4.0","nsPath":"/","ciGoid":"100-1085-57129","comments":null,"ciState":"default","lastAppl
iedRfcId":0,"createdBy":"oneops","updatedBy":"oneops","created":1450470777810,"updated":1
450470814468,"nsId":100,"ciAttributes":{"owner":"admin@oneops.com","full_name":"OneOps gr
oup","description":""},"attrProps":{}}
[root@ip-172-31-57-184 ~]#
```

Use the `oneops auth login` command to log in. Once logged in, you can set the `organization` to your default organization. Remember that the CLI will not allow you to do anything that the GUI does not allow you to do. Running OneOps help will provide you with help on the commands that you can run from the OneOps CLI:

```
    General
    -------
      version           Display OneOps CLI gem version.
      help [<command>]  Display this help or help for a particular command.

    Setup & Configuration
    ---------------------
      config            Set or display global parameters (e.g. login, password, host, def
ault assembly).

    OneOps Management Commands
    --------------------------
      account           Account management.
      organization      Organization management.
      cloud             Cloud management.
      catalog           Catalog management.
      assembly          Assembly management.
      design            Assembly design management.
      transition        Assembly transition management.
      operations        Assmebly operations management.

For more information about commands try:
    oneops help <command>
[root@ip-172-31-57-184 ~]# 
```

Once you are logged in, you can run all kinds of commands to get details on existing components, such as your organization, assemblies, catalog, clouds, and so on. You can even query your assembly to see the constituent pack components and can even transition the assembly from the command-line tool:

```
[root@ip-172-31-57-184 ~]# oneops cloud
[{"ciId":57143,"ciName":"aws-east-1","ciClassName":"account.Cloud","impl":"oo::chef-11.4.
0","nsPath":"/OneOps/_clouds","ciGoid":"57142-1013-57143","comments":"","ciState":"defaul
t","lastAppliedRfcId":0,"createdBy":"oneops","updatedBy":null,"created":1452036157866,"up
dated":1452036157866,"nsId":57142,"ciAttributes":{"adminstatus":"active","auth":"","descr
iption":"","location":"/public/oneops/clouds/ec2-us-east-1"},"attrProps":{}}]
[root@ip-172-31-57-184 ~]# oneops design show -a SimpleApache

Platforms:
  Name                    Pack              Description
  --------------------    --------------    ----------------------------------------
  webapp                  apache

Current Release: 2585 (closed) created by oneops on 2016-01-11 17:40:45 +0000.
  Committed by oneops 2016-01-11 17:40:51 +0000.
  Description:
[root@ip-172-31-57-184 ~]# oneops design packs -a SimpleApache
[{"oneops":{"mysql":["1"],"activemq":["1"],"customlb":["1"],"apache":["1"],"java":["1"],"
rabbitmq":["1"],"cassandra":["1"],"couchbase":["1"],"custom":["1"],"es":["1"],"javaws":["
1"],"ruby":["1"],"tomcat":["1"],"haproxy":["1"],"rails":["1"],"postgresql":["1"],"gluster
fs":["1"],"php":["1"],"oneops":["1"],"inductor":["1"]}}]
[root@ip-172-31-57-184 ~]#
```

Control OneOps from command line

You can even get operations information on an assembly and perform an **ops** operation on an assembly via the command `oneops operations`.

Summary

In this chapter, we saw an in depth view of the OneOps architecture. We saw various backend components and their functions and how they work together to provide various services that, as a whole, form OneOps. We also saw some useful utilities that give us some insight into the backend data and make the management of the data and the system easier. So far, we have been dealing with single system OneOps installations.

In the next chapter, we will take a look at enterprise installation of OneOps and various things that you will have to consider when you wish to deploy OneOps on an enterprise-wide level.

3
OneOps Application Life Cycle

In the previous chapters, you learned ways to install OneOps on a single server using various methods. By now, you are familiar with the various cogs and wheels that make up OneOps. In this chapter, we will start configuring OneOps, so you can do actual deployments of applications and monitor them post deployment. However, before you can start doing deployments, you need to configure and prepare your OneOps setup for deployments. For this, you will need to configure your targets, such as clouds, services, and so on. So, let's first take a look at how to do it.

Adding a cloud to your organization

As mentioned in Chapter 1, *Getting Started with OneOps*, the first thing you had to do after installing OneOps was to create an organization. Remember that the term organization is used to just logically group your resources. So, if you work for a small company, you may very well group all your resources under one organization. If, however, you work for a big company, you may decide to create one organization per department. If your company departments are also too big, you may have decided to have an organization per team inside of that department, so you can manage the allocation of team, resources, clouds, and services better. The decision is entirely up to you, and it should be planned carefully. However, after you have added your organization and arranged your team members, you will have to add a cloud and then add services to the cloud before you can start doing deployments.

Click on **Clouds** on the left-hand side menu, and you will be taken to the cloud addition page. If you are trying the Amazon AMI and logged in with the username *oneops* and password *oneops*, you will note a cloud named **ec2-cloud**, which is an excellent and descriptive name, has already been added for you to quickly get you up and running. If you click on the cloud, you will see various attributes, as well as various services added to the cloud:

If you are starting with a brand new blank installation, click on the **Add Cloud** button or link. This will take you to a screen, which will allow you to add a cloud. Choose a good descriptive name for your cloud, as in the preceding example, and add a good description. Then, choose the cloud location. At the time of writing this, OneOps supports AWS, Azure, Rackspace, and OpenStack (custom) clouds. Although Vagrant and Docker are listed as cloud targets, they are placeholders for future expansions and are not valid targets at the moment. If you wish to deploy one of the existing clouds, such as AWS, Azure, Rackspace, or OpenStack, it is important that you choose **Location** carefully as OneOps will configure a few things automatically for you:

 If you define a cloud of the type **Custom**, you will also be asked to provide an authorization key. This authorization key will be used when you connect your services to a backend inductor.

Once you have configured a cloud, it will be an umbrella under which you will configure various services which you will use then for deployments. It is not necessary, as we will soon see, to have all the services from the same vendor, which is the beauty of OneOps. You can also configure multiple clouds and use them in a redundant fashion to deploy your software at the same time to multiple locations. Once you have added your cloud, all your clouds will show up in the clouds section, as shown in the following screenshot:

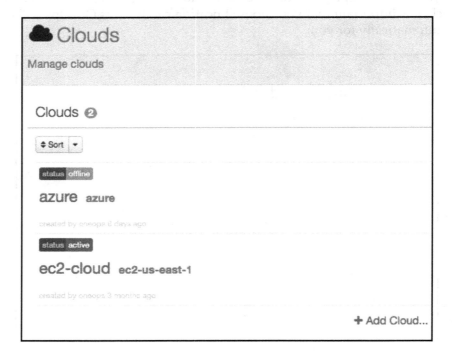

Now you are ready to add services to your cloud.

A brief note on services

As mentioned earlier, a cloud is an umbrella that groups various services together. To successfully deploy an application to a cloud, it is necessary to have a few services. Without these services, your OneOps will not be able to deploy your application, or your application will not function properly. Before we see how to add services, let's have a brief look at the type of services you need to add to a cloud.

Compute

Compute is the primary service that you will add to the cloud, on top of which an application will be deployed. In terms of most clouds, this will translate to the virtual machines of various sizes that are available, to which your application will be deployed. Compute capacity can be provided by Azure, Amazon AWS, Rackspace, OpenStack, Docker, and Vagrant. OpenStack, Docker, and Vagrant can be your own local clouds.

 At the time of writing, Docker and Vagrant are not supported as compute options, but will be supported soon, in a future release.

DNS

A **DNS** service is needed for your application to be identified globally and in an easy manner. We will take a look at the application naming convention at the time of application deployment, however, OneOps does not like to rely on the name provided by the cloud provider for various reasons. Firstly, the **vm** deployed underneath your application may need to be replaced at anytime, in which case, it is easy to do so if it has a DNS record pointing to it. Secondly, if the application is deployed in a load-balanced way, then a DNS must be used, which OneOps will configure to the load-balancer. Thirdly, if you deploy a redundant setup on two or more different clouds, then it makes it is easier for OneOps to switch to the backup application if the primary goes down if you have the DNS setup. Hence, adding DNS service to your cloud is mandatory.

 DNS is not the same as your normal DNS service, but what is normally referred to as a Cloud DNS service provided by Amazon Route 53, Rackspace DNS. If you have a domain name, these services let you manage that domain via an API.

Global DNS

Global DNS (GDNS), acts as a traffic router on a global level. It routes traffic based on your DNS records on a global level. If you have deployments in multiple zones or multiple data centers, then GDNS can make your apps more responsive by routing traffic to the nearest zone for your clients. Currently, OneOps supports Azure, Azure Traffic Manager, AWS Route 53, and Rackspace GDNS.

Load balancer

Load balancers are used to make applications fault-tolerant across multiple instances and availability zones. Load balancers are also used to remove unhealthy VMs from application pools. Currently, OneOps supports Azure, AWS (ELB), OpenStack (Neutron), and Rackspace load balancers.

Storage

Storage is external block storage that can be attached to individual VMs. The only service currently supported is Amazon's EBS and Azure's data disk. Since block storage consists of vendor specific storage devices, they can only be attached if the compute instances are spun on that vendor's cloud services; that is, you can attach Azure data disk to your instances only if your compute instances are on Azure.

File store

The only **file store** currently supported is **Amazon Simple Storage System** (**Amazon S3**), which is a highly available object store good for storing files, images, and logs.

Adding services under your cloud

Now that you have a general idea of what services are and what they do, let's add some services to your cloud. Click on your cloud and click on **Add Service**. You will be given a drop-down box with options to add various types of services. Let's start by adding an AWS compute service.

Adding a compute service

Select the region you want to add. Currently supported regions are **US-East-1**, **US-West-1**, and **US-West-2**. The minimal configuration you will have to provide is **Access Key*** and **Secret Key***, as follows:

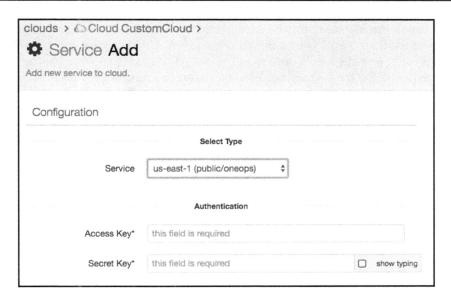

To get the access key, go to your AWS console and select **IAM** (short for **Identity Access Management**). It is recommended that you create a new user and then generate new credentials for it. You get to access these credentials only once, however, you do get the option to download them. It is highly recommended that you download these credentials, as you will be using these credentials in various places. It is also recommended that you keep these credentials in a very secure place as they, depending on the accesses granted, will allow the user access to various AWS services via the AWS API.

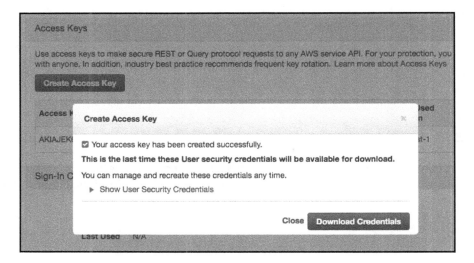

If you are adding a Rackspace compute service, then your tenant name and username are your Rackspace username and your password is your Rackspace password. For the OpenStack compute engine, Nova, tenant name is also the same as your username and a password is required for the username. You also need to know the API endpoint for NOVA.

Adding Azure compute (or any) services is a bit involved. Firstly, you must have an Azure account. Once you have an Azure account, you will need to sign in to the Azure portal and add Azure Active Directory Service. Once you add **Active Directory** to your Azure Account, click on **Application** and add your OneOps application. Azure will ask you to add **App ID** and **App URL**. The **App URL** has to be a valid OneOps installation URL, although it can be on your intranet. Once you click on **Configure**, you will see all the details that you will need to add to OneOps screen. You will see the **client ID**, and you will also be able to generate the secret keys.

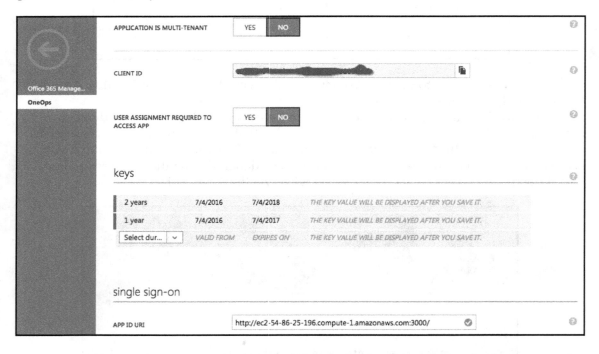

To get your Azure Subscription ID, click on **subscriptions** on the left-hand side menu and select the subscription you are using. You will see your subscription IDs listed on the right.

Adding a DNS service

To add a DNS service, you should have an account with either one or all of the major cloud providers, or have a cloud installation of your own such, as OpenStack. The keys you have used so far are the same for AWS, Azure, and OpenStack, with the exception of Rackspace. Rackspace is also the easiest DNS service to configure. So, if you are testing the Vagrant installation or the AWS AMI, then you can try it out with the Rackspace DNS (which is free), along with a free domain name provider. Go ahead and add Rackspace DNS to your cloud with the relevant details:

Just for Rackspace DNS, instead of password, OneOps will ask you to enter an **API Key**. You will find the API key in **Rackspace settings**. Click on **Show** and it will show you the API key. Copy and paste the API key. On the Rackspace side, make sure that you click on **Networking** and then **DNS**, and add your **Domain Name** record. If you are using Amazon Route 53, adding it is the same as adding the EC2 compute. Just make sure that, on the Amazon side, either you buy a domain or, if you are managing an existing domain, you create an appropriate hosted zone. You will also be asked to provide a zone and a cloud ID. Choose an ID appropriate for a zone, which can be a unique string or a geographical ID. For the cloud ID, use a unique identifying string.

Adding a GDNS service

Adding a GDNS service is pretty much the same as adding a DNS service. You will be asked pretty much the same value from the same vendors. Even for zones and cloud ID, you can choose the same values, unless you are deploying in production. In this case, you will want to configure different redundancy zones for your DNS.

 Once your DNS is configured, it may take as much as 24 hours for the DNS changes to propagate all over the world. Until then, your deployments might fail or give you strange errors.

Adding a storage service

After adding compute and DNS, you may want to add a storage service. However, this is only needed if your cloud is on AWS, and is not compulsory. The steps are the same as adding any service on Amazon and the details you will need to enter are also exactly the same.

Adding load balancer

It is always a good idea to deploy your app behind a load balancer, especially for a web-based app. A load balancer, in conjunction with your GDNS, will ensure that your app is always serving a proper load. This also makes it easy to scale up the app if it experiences a heavy volume and scale it down again once the volume subsides. The steps to add a load balancer are the same as adding other corresponding services from the providers with the exact same details required.

Adding a mirror service

When you install an application such as Apache Webserver, Apache Tomcat, or MySQL, sometimes OneOps downloads them from the Internet. For this reason, OneOps maintains the links to the latest stable versions of these and other software in a service named mirror service. To get access to these links, you need to add a mirror service to the cloud. Although you can customize it and add more locations to it, for now, you can simply leave it as is and use the defaults.

After this, your cloud is ready to receive some deployments.

Designing an assembly

As mentioned before, an assembly represents your application in its entirety. It has all the information needed to spawn, scale, and monitor your application. This includes the compute instance needed, OS and other software on top of it, the application software, FQDN, security groups, SSH keys, and any other software that needs to be installed as part of the deployment. Click on the assembly link on the left-hand side menu and you will see your current assemblies as follows:

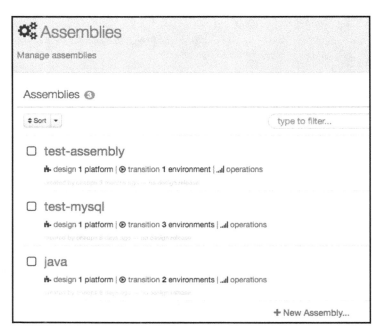

The first column under the assembly name tells you how many platforms or software packages are part of the assembly. In the preceding example, Java has one platform as part of it, which is JDK 1.7. The second column tells you which environments it was transitioned to. The preceding example tells you that Java was transitioned to two environments. The third column is a handy link to operations, from where you view notifications and perform various operations.

Now, let's create a simple assembly to deploy: a simple VM with JDK installed on it that will be deployed on the cloud that we designed earlier. Click on the **New Assembly** link to start creating a new assembly. Let's call the assembly `test-java`. Give it a good description, and in the e-mail ID field, provide your e-mail ID. In the future, if and when you turn on monitoring, all alerts will go to this e-mail ID:

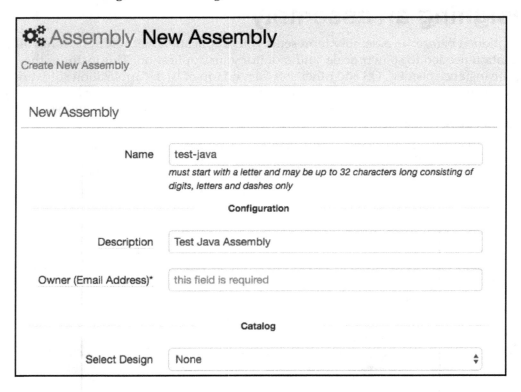

Now, there won't be any preexisting designs to choose from. So, simply click on **OK**. You have just created your first assembly, however, there is nothing inside of it, as it's just an empty box. So, let's fill it with useful information and instructions. Since we want to install JDK on VM, let's select Java from the platforms on the right-hand side. Give it a name, say **JDK**. Remember that no spaces are allowed. Provide a description and, from the OneOps pack, add Java:

Now, before we see the magic that is OneOps, it helps to reiterate its purpose. OneOps is a multi-cloud management software. Hence, even by the simple act of adding Java to your assembly, OneOps makes some intelligent assumptions about your deployment. These assumptions are of course customizable.

However, out-of-the-box they work well and they are best practices. You will immediately note that, besides Java, OneOps has added a few other things to your assembly. OneOps adds a compute instance, a security group to control access to and from the compute instance, an OS instance on which OneOps will install and customize the software, and lastly, a **Fully Qualified Domain Name** (**FQDN**) that will be reachable from anywhere, depending on your configuration:

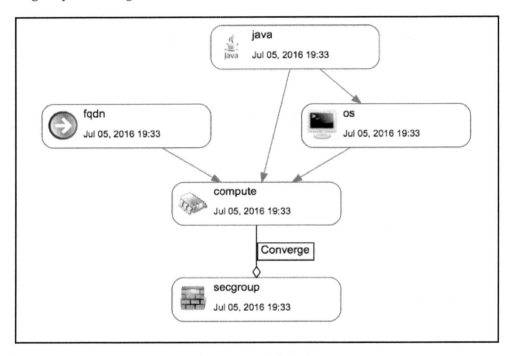

So, even if you are deploying just a VM with Java on it, it is still a secure VM that is ready to run enterprise-level apps. Now, before we deploy the assembly, let's tweak a few settings. Click on **Design** on the left-hand menu till you see the preceding diagram. Then, click on the image that says **Compute**. Change the size of compute from **Small** to **Micro**. There is no particular reason for doing this besides to demonstrate how to tweak various settings in various aspects of your assembly. Also, because this is a test assembly, we don't really need a small instance. Micro will do fine and will boot up faster:

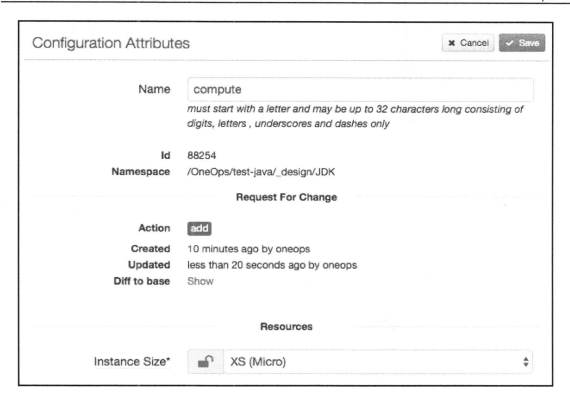

Of course, after we deploy the whole assembly, we would also like to SSH to our new VM to verify that the deployment went fine. For this purpose, we will create a user in advance and insert it into our assembly. Again, click on **design** on the left-hand side and click on the **Platform Name** (test-java). You will see that all the components are available on the right-hand side and the components that have already been inserted are expanded, with the number of components inserted displayed in a small circle. For example, because we have one computing instance and one OS instance in our assembly, you will see both of them expanded and they will have a small **1** next to them.

Find a component named **User** and click on the plus sign next to it. This will bring you to the **User Add** screen. Pick a good username, a home directory, and a default shell. You will also need an SSH key. If you do not have one, it is highly recommended that you create one with ssh-keygen and keep your private key secure. Copy and paste your public key into the authorized key field:

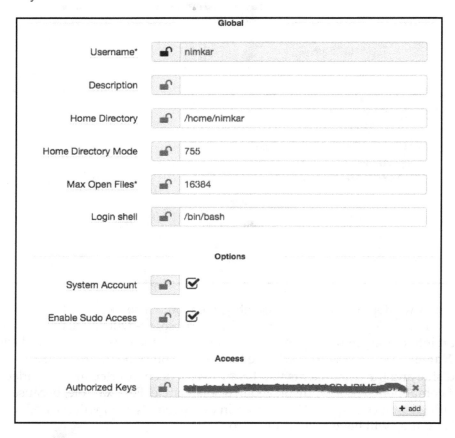

Those are all the changes needed for now. Click on **Commit**. Commit allows you to save the changes made to the assembly. OneOps also versions all the changes you make with every commit. So, should you make any breaking changes, you always have the option of going back to a previous commit and deploying again, thus undoing any catastrophe. Now your assembly is ready for deployment and we have a cloud all ready to receive deployments. Next, let's create an environment to deploy an assembly.

Create an environment and deploy your assembly

An environment is an intersection of your assembly and a cloud. You will attach a cloud to your assembly to create an environment. As your assembly progresses through different environments, you can go on attaching either different or the same cloud with a different name to the assembly to deploy it. Thus, you will want to create descriptive names, which clearly state their purpose, such as development, QA, staging, production, and so on. Depending on how you deploy your assembly, the environment name also gets appended to the FQDN and will become part of how you address your server or call your app, so how you pick your environment name is crucial. Go ahead and click on **Transition** on the left-hand side and then click on **New Environment** on the screen. Let's call this environment **Dev**:

You can set the administrative status as **Provision** for now, which means your app is being provisioned. However, if you are confident that the deployment will go forth without error, then you can also set it to active. As you can see, OneOps has already generated a subdomain for you based on a combination of environment, assembly, and organization. This subdomain will be appended to the domain name that you configured to make your app accessible. For this test, I had registered a domain named practicalops.tk. This means my test Java deployment will be accessible at Dev.test-java.OneOps.practicalops.tk.

.tk, .ml, and lots of other kinds of domains can be registered for free (at least for 90 days) on various sites. One good site is http://www.freenom.com/en/index.html?lang=en. You can use it along with Rackspace DNS (which is also free) to run all kinds of tests.

Because my installation has only one organization, that is OneOps, I can uncheck the **organization** box. In this case, after deployment, my application will be accessible at Dev.test-java.practicalops.tk. Go ahead and **commit** your changes. You are now ready to deploy your assembly. Click on **deploy**. Once you click on **deploy**, OneOps will generate a deployment plan. You will get a chance to review it and back out if necessary. If all looks in order, go ahead and click on **deploy** again. OneOps will now start the deployment step-by-step. Depending on the steps, it may take some time.

You can view the logs by clicking on a particular step, expanding it, and clicking on the log link:

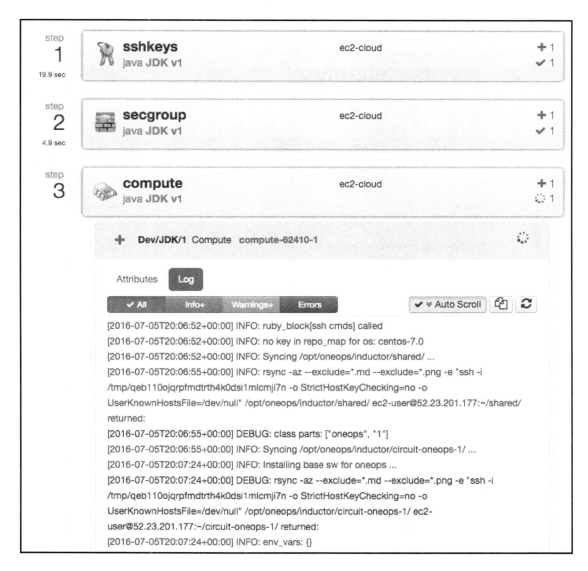

Once an assembly is deployed successfully, you can click on the **assembly name** on the left-hand side and see the status of the deployment at any time. Examples shown later are statuses of various deployments of an assembly named **test-mysql**, which is very similar to test-java but has a MySQL database deployed on it and also has block storage attached to it:

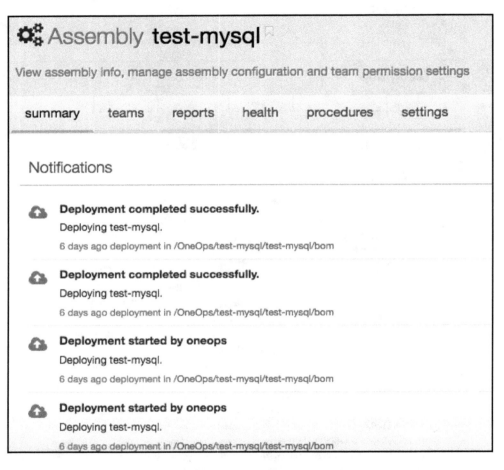

You can also view various reports and the health of your assembly by clicking on the **health** and **reports** tabs. The **reports** tab will show you details such as how many cores are used by your applications, whereas the **health** tab will show you the overall health of your assembly.

Monitoring your assembly

When you deploy your assembly, some default monitors are attached to it to keep it healthy. If you click on the assembly name and see the **Environments** tab to the right, you will see the autorepair tag already attached to successful deployments. What this means is, if something goes wrong with your assembly, OneOps will automatically try to repair your assembly by taking the appropriate measures to a certain degree. These measures fall short, however, of replacing the whole application. That does not happen unless autoreplace is enabled. To support features such as auto repair and autoreplace, OneOps comes with some powerful monitoring tools built in. You can click on any deployed assembly and then click on the health tab to see everything that is being monitored. By default, you will only see alerts. However, if you want to see all the components, then select the good instances and you will be able to see all the components of the assembly that are being monitored. You can also tweak alerts to your liking. For example, let's say, in the preceding example, you want to alert when 90% of the disk space is used on the attached storage on MySQL. Click on the **Attached Volume** component and Click on **Monitors**. You will see that the **Usage monitor** is active for the **Volume** component. In the top right-hand corner, you will see an **edit** button. Click on it. Scroll down, and you will see **Alerting**. Select the **Heartbeat** checkbox. Click on the **LowDiskSpace** button and change the state from **Notify** to **Unhealthy**. Note that the trigger state is above 90% and the reset state is below 90%. You can also tweak the duration, occurrence, and cool-off period:

Just as the storage component has a custom monitor, most of the components supplied by OneOps have monitors that can be customized too.

Summary

In this chapter, we saw how to define our cloud, what exactly comprises a cloud, and how to add and define services for our cloud. We also saw how to define an assembly and add components to it. We also defined environments for an assembly and successfully transitioned an assembly through the environment. We finally added some monitoring to the assembly. All of this was done using a single installation of OneOps. In the next chapter, we will take a look at some suggestions for an enterprise-level installation of OneOps.

4

OneOps Enterprise Deployment

In the previous chapters, you saw ways to install OneOps on a single server using various methods. You also saw a detailed overview of the OneOps architecture. Running OneOps on a single server serves well for development, demonstration, and proof-of-concept purposes. However, for a true enterprise-level setup, different OneOps services should be installed on different servers to better handle the enterprise-level load. It is very important to understand not only the architecture of OneOps, but also the reasoning behind it. At Walmart itself, OneOps allowed them to go from one or two large monolithic deployments once every two months to about 1000 deployments per typical development day. Of course, this turnaround was not achieved by simply installing OneOps. It took a huge effort that involved restructuring current applications with service-oriented architecture. Walmart also embraced DevOps culture and provided ownership and accountability of infrastructure for each service that a developer releases. They achieved this by the ALM model provided by OneOps, where it bundles infrastructure as part of the application. Lastly, Walmart provided its developers easy access to infrastructure by abstracting and bundling the infrastructure as part of the definition of the deployment via OneOps. Thus, developers were free to code and could rest assured their code could be deployed to any cloud infrastructure that OneOps would hook into.

Considerations for enterprise-level installation

OneOps is a DevOps automation tool. As such, your first consideration for the implementation of OneOps should be the implementation of DevOps in your enterprise. Is your company already practicing DevOps? Is it ready to handle DevOps? The allure of DevOps success tempts many companies to dive head first into DevOps tool implementations without giving due thought to the DevOps culture itself. This has given rise to more DevOps failures than success stories. Before you install any enterprise-level DevOps tool, do a careful evaluation of your processes and practices and see how it will affect your development workflow.

OneOps is geared to deliver many benefits to your organization. However, you can take full advantage of those benefits only if the processes in your organization are aligned to do so. Following are a few things you may want to consider before you move to a more DevOps-oriented process:

- Train your developers on *Infrastructure as a Service* model. Train them on how they can request, scale, and dispose their own infrastructure on the fly.
- Make developers responsible for their own applications. This includes design, build, package, and deploy, all the way to production. This should also include monitoring in production and responding to production events.
- If you have a dedicated operations team, plan the synergy between operations and development. It's OK to have some overlap, provided it is permitted by governance.
- Refactor your code. Start breaking down your monolithic applications into smaller components. Start moving towards microservice architecture. The smaller the application, the more rapidly you will be able to deploy it.
- Plan and segregate your environments beforehand. You may want to have dedicated clouds or zones for development, QA, and production. Control access accordingly.
- Giving more access to developers in areas where they did not previously have access will increase productivity. However, traceability, accountability, and responsibility are also important. So, be sure to strike a balance.
- Rapid deployments may or may not always translate into productivity. Don't impose a rapid deployment schedule. That defeats the purpose of DevOps. Take input from all stakeholder teams, such as development, QA, and Ops and come up with a schedule that works for everyone. From there, let the schedule evolve organically with the code and the teams.

This is by no means a comprehensive list, but it gives you an idea that, if an enterprise wishes to transition to DevOps and implement a tool like OneOps, then technical considerations are not the only points that it has to worry about. Of course, each organization will have a list of their own processes and policies. However, a comprehensive discussion of DevOps processes is beyond the scope of this book.

Tips and suggestions for enterprise-level installation

Since this book is about practical OneOps, we will focus on the practical aspects of enterprise-level OneOps installation. As we saw in Chapter 2, *Understanding the OneOps Architecture*, OneOps is a complex piece of software with a lot of moving parts. Pretty much each of the services or components translates into a server or installation. Installing and configuring each service individually is a difficult, if not impossible, task. Fortunately, the OneOps team has already automated the enterprise installation for you. The best way to install and manage OneOps in an enterprise is to use OneOps to install OneOps. In Chapter 1, *Getting Started with OneOps*, we saw how to install a Vagrant instance to install a test instance of OneOps. You can use a Vagrant instance of OneOps to perform an enterprise-level installation. However, if your OneOps instance will be running on a public cloud like AWS or Azure, I generally recommend your initial instance should be running on the same cloud too. This is not necessary, but just convenient. If you want to do your enterprise installation on AWS, you already know how to bring up a OneOps instance from the Amazon AMI. However, it brings up OneOps with slightly older code, which you will have to update manually (covered in Chapter 6, *Managing Your OneOps*). However, if you want to deploy on Azure or Rackspace, or your own internal cloud, such as OpenStack, then you have no choice but to go with a Vagrant install. Fortunately using the same Vagrant scripts, you can quickly bootstrap a OneOps installation in the cloud. Simply follow the instructions below. The below instructions are for AWS, but should work equally well on Azure, Rackspace, or OpenStack.

Start with a CentOS 7 instance, if possible. On Amazon, just go to the AWS Marketplace and search for CentOS 7. The very first result you see should be for the official CentOS 7 AMI. Select that AMI, as shown following.

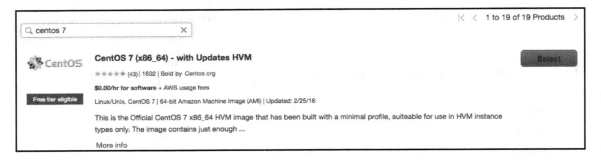

Click the big blue **Select** button and, on the next screen, select at least**m4.large** instance. It has at least 2 vCPUs and 8 GB of memory. The more memory and vCPUs your instance has, the better the performance. After that, follow the instructions in `Chapter 1`, *Getting Started with OneOps*, to bring up a working instance of CentOS. Once you have a working instance of CentOS up and running, it will be a bare-bones install without anything running on it at all. Start by installing `git` on it. We require `git` because, in the next step, we will be checking out the OneOps setup repository from GitHub, which will help us bootstrap OneOps.

```
sudo yum install git
```

After installing `git` `clone` the latest version of OneOps setup repository, preferably in the CentOS home directory `/home/centos`.

```
git clone https://github.com/oneops/setup.git
```

Now you should have a directory called `setup`. Under that directory, you should have a directory called `vagrant-centos7`, as shown in the following screenshot.

```
[centos@ip-172-31-52-21 ~]$ ls
setup
[centos@ip-172-31-52-21 ~]$ cd setup
[centos@ip-172-31-52-21 setup]$ ls
design  docker  README.md  vagrant  vagrant-centos7
[centos@ip-172-31-52-21 setup]$ cd vagrant-centos7/
[centos@ip-172-31-52-21 vagrant-centos7]$ ls
amq        display  logstash     oo-setup.sh  search-consumer  Vagrantfile
cassandra  git_ssh  oo-prereqs.sh  pgsql        tomcat
[centos@ip-172-31-52-21 vagrant-centos7]$ ls oo-prereqs.sh oo-setup.sh
oo-prereqs.sh  oo-setup.sh
[centos@ip-172-31-52-21 vagrant-centos7]$
```

Under that directory are two scripts that can be used to bootstrap an instance of OneOps. `oo-prereqs.sh` and `oo-setup.sh`. Open the first script, called `oo-prereqs.sh`. This script will install all the prerequisites for a working OneOps instance on a single server. This includes Ruby, JDK, Perl, Postgres, ActiveMQ, Cassandra, Tomcat, Maven, Elasticsearch, and Logstash, among a ton of other things. Before you can run that script, open it and change the variable `VAGRANT_MNT` at the top of the script to point to the current directory.

```sh
#!/bin/sh

now=$(date +"%T")
echo "Starting at : $now"

export VAGRANT_MNT="/home/centos/setup/vagrant-centos7"

echo '127.0.0.1    localhost localhost.localdomain localhost4 localhost4.localdom
ain4 search api antenna opsmq daq opsdb sysdb kloopzappdb kloopzcmsdb cmsapi sen
sor activitidb kloopzmq searchmq' > /etc/hosts
echo '::1          localhost localhost.localdomain localhost6 localhost6.localdom
ain6' >> /etc/hosts

# disable ruby doc, this would speed up the install while a bit
echo 'gem: --no-document' >> ~/.gemrc

# java
echo "00 installing open jdk 1.8"
yum -y install java-1.8.0-openjdk-devel

# misc
yum -y install git wget vim-common ntp perl-Digest-SHA
systemctl enable ntpd
```

After you have changed the directory, just run the script. Remember, you may have to give execute permission to the script. You also have to run the script with `root` permission. You can either do this with `sudo`, or you can just go ahead and log in as `root` with the following command:

```
sudo su -
```

The script will download all the prerequisites from the Internet and install and configure them where necessary. Once all the prerequisites are installed, you can run the second script, `oo-setup.sh`, which will install the actual OneOps software. Again, this script has to be run as `root`. If you run this script without any parameters, it will build and install the last stable build. Since we will be using this instance to bootstrap an enterprise OneOps installation in the cloud, it is advisable to install a master build, instead of the last stable build which may not have all the latest changes.

In terms of development, OneOps follows the agile model. Hence, commits to master are very frequent, whereas a stable tag is not so frequent. A build from master gives you access to features that won't make it to the stable branch for a few months.

Use the following command to install the latest `master` build. You can always rerun this command to update your OneOps build to the latest on the master or any branch.

```
./oo-setup.sh master
```

This will run a complete OneOps setup, including the building and installing of OneOps code, installing, migrating and populating of OneOps databases, stopping and starting of services, and so on. Once the script is done running, your instance in cloud is primed and ready to install an enterprise installation. The only thing remaining to do is to tune your security groups to allow access to the web port 3000. Remember, Display is a Ruby on Rails application and, hence, runs on port 3000. You can also access port 8080 if you want to debug or want to connect to **cms-admin**.

Type ⓘ	Protocol ⓘ	Port Range ⓘ	Source ⓘ
Custom TCP Rule	TCP	8080	0.0.0.0/0
SSH	TCP	22	0.0.0.0/0
Custom TCP Rule	TCP	3000	0.0.0.0/0

You now have a OneOps instance in the cloud, built with the latest code, all primed to install an enterprise instance of OneOps.

Using OneOps to install OneOps

Now, as mentioned in previous chapters, access your instance at port 3000. Register a convenient user name with an accessible e-mail ID and log in as that user. Create an organization with a name you want. For this example, I called mine OneOps. Now click on assemblies on the left-hand side and click on **New Assembly**. This is the assembly that is going to install your enterprise OneOps system. Let's call this OneOps too. Now, on your laptop or desktop or wherever you are doing this from, clone a copy of the OneOps setup repository again.

```
git clone https://github.com/oneops/setup.git
```

Once the repository is checked out along with the vagrant directories, you will also see a directory called design. This directory contains the OneOps design definitions. Click on the empty assembly that you created, called **OneOps**, and then click on **design** on the left-hand side menu. On the top right-hand side, you will see four buttons, **Extract**, **Load**, **Copy**, and, **Save to Catalog**. Click on **Load**. This will take you to a page that will ask you to either copy and paste the YAML definition of the assembly, or else load the YAML from a file. Click on the big blue **Choose a File** button. Navigate to the design directory and choose the file called `oneops-design.YAML`. If you scroll down, you will see the option to either just validate the design or load it, as shown following:

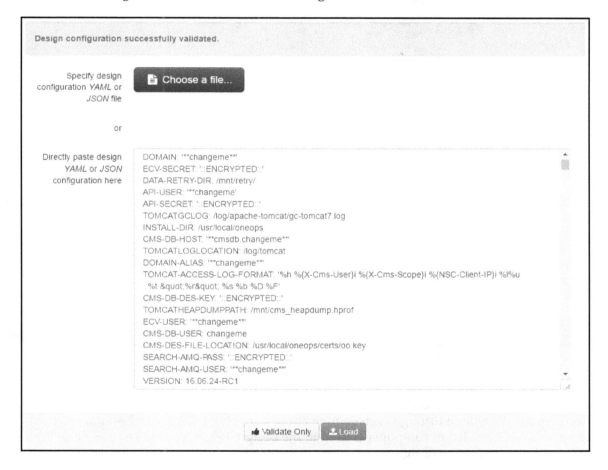

If you validate the design, it will load the YAML into the text area below and also validate the design for you. You can then load the design by clicking **Load**.

 Ain't Markup Language or **Yet Another Markup Language** (**YAML**) depending on who you ask. It is a human-readable data serializable language primarily favored by Python and Somewhat by Ruby. OneOps also supports JSON.

Once you click **Load**, OneOps will load the design and show you the standard design diagram view of the OneOps architecture.

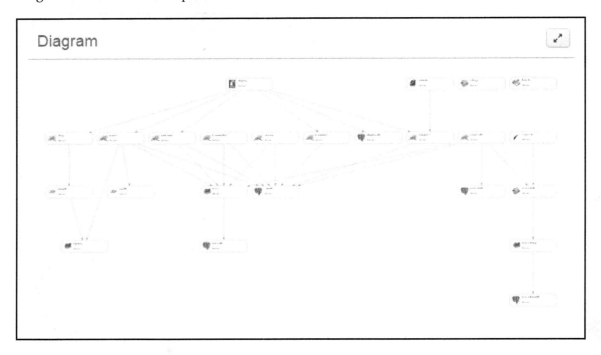

The design is big and complicated, hence the individual components are too tiny to see. You can click on the arrows on the upper right-hand side to expand to fullscreen. However, unless you have a huge monitor, the individual components will still be too tiny to see. Fortunately, we will go through each component in detail here. On the right-hand side, you can also see the full list of components used in the design. Before you do anything else, it's a good idea to commit the design.

The first thing you can do, before you do a deep dive into the design, is to customize the installation. You can do this by changing the variables associated with the design.

OneOps uses variables to define various key-value pairs that it can replace dynamically during deployment time. You can define values for keys at various levels and those values are then replaced for those corresponding keys when OneOps deploys your assembly. OneOps defines variables at global, cloud, and local level. Global variables are accessible throughout the assembly, cloud variables are accessible only to a particular cloud, and local variables are accessible to only a particular platform.

Click on **Design** and then on the variables tab to see all the variables defined by the OneOps assembly. On the left, you will see all the variables defined by OneOps. If you click on a particular variable, you will see the current value of the variable. If you mark it as a secure variable, it will be encrypted for you and the value will not be displayed. The right-hand side will also display some more useful data about the variable, such as it's ID, namespace, and a history of changes.

Before you begin the installation, you can tune various global variables to customize your installation and make it more secure. You may consider changing the values of the following variables. However, you will have to go through quite some customization of the whole OneOps design before you can deploy a working OneOps enterprise system.

- **AMQDBUSER**: The default username used by AMQ is **amqdb**. This is a very common username and you may consider changing it to something that is not so obvious for security reasons. This username will trickle down and will be used by all OneOps components to connect to AMQ.

- **AMQDBPASS**: Set this to something secure. Remember OneOps encrypts this information so there is no way of knowing what the password was, should you forget it. You may have to run the installation again or change the password manually for the components should this happen.
- **ACTIVITI-DB-PASS**: Again, change this to something secure and remember what you set it to. It's a good idea not to set all the passwords to the same password. Each application, database, and queue should have a different secure password.
- **DISTBASE**: This is the repository from where OneOps will install its builds. Currently, OneOps assumes it's a Nexus repository, but it can be any repository with URL or file-based access. The assumption here is, since you are installing an enterprise grade OneOps system, you will also install a continuous integration and Nexus-like repository to take advantage of rapid code changes that are made to the OneOps code base. An internal system also helps you leverage your own development efforts and send pull requests to the master OneOps codebase on GitHub.
- **CMS-DB-PASS**: This is the password used to connect to the CMS database. Change this to something secure and unique.
- **AMQPASS**: This is the password used to connect to AMQ. This is the actual queue, not to be confused with the AMQ Database.
- **DOMAIN**: Your enterprise domain name, under which you will be releasing your apps and under which your clouds reside. Plan this carefully. This can be `yourcompany.com`, `yourcompany.net` or something similar.
- **ECV-USER**: This is the user that will be configured and used to send various commands to all the Tomcat instances when they are stopped, started, and restarted. Change this to a unique username.
- **ECV-SECRET**: Change this to a secure string. This, along with **ECV-USER**, is used to control Tomcat monitoring. **Extended Content Verification** (ECV) is to verify the health of Tomcat and report various health events on Tomcat.

- **SEARCHMQDBPASSWORD**: This is the password for the postgres database that acts as a datastore for the search queue. Again, change it to something secure.
- **API-USER**: This is the user that will be used to run various commands against OneOps via the OneOps API. You will have to create this user in OneOps and grant it appropriate permissions after you assign a value to this variable.
- **API-SECRET**: After you create the above user, assign a secret string to uniquely identify the user.
- **CMS-DB-HOST**: This is the hostname for your CMSDB. Replace this with the **FQDN** where your **CMSDB** will reside.
- **DOMAIN-ALIAS**: Replace this with any alias that your domains might have. If your company uses an internal naming convention, this is a good place to define it.
- **CMS-DB-USER**: The username that will be used to access CMSDB. Change this to something unique and secure.
- **SEARCH-AMQ-USER**: This is the username used to connect to the search queue. Change this to something unique and secure.
- **VERSION**: The version of OneOps that will be installed. Choose a stable version for installation; since this will be an enterprise installation, installing from the master branch is not a good idea.
- **BACKUP-HOST**: This is the host where postgres backups will be stored. Change it to a hostname which has redundancy, good backup retention, and that gets backed up to other backup mediums periodically, like tape.

As mentioned previously, the master branch for OneOps is frequently committed to. A stable tag, on the other hand, is extensively tested and very stable. Hence, to manage your enterprise infrastructure, you should always deploy off a stable tag.

Once the global variable customization is done, we can now look at each OneOps component and customize some of them for installation. OneOps has a total of 23 components that it will install as part of the enterprise install. Almost every component is installed on it's own instance. Many, if not most of them, have already been covered in Chapter 2, *Understanding the OneOps Architecture*. For a running OneOps enterprise installation you don't need to customize each and every component. We will go through the ones that you do need to customize.

Display

Display is the web frontend for OneOps, written in Ruby on Rails. The display application runs as user `ooadmin` on an Apache HTTPD server. It installs Ruby on Rails. The actual display application is installed from the Nexus repository defined in the global variable DISTBASE. Display connects directly to daq, transistor, displaydb, adapter, antenna, and sensor.

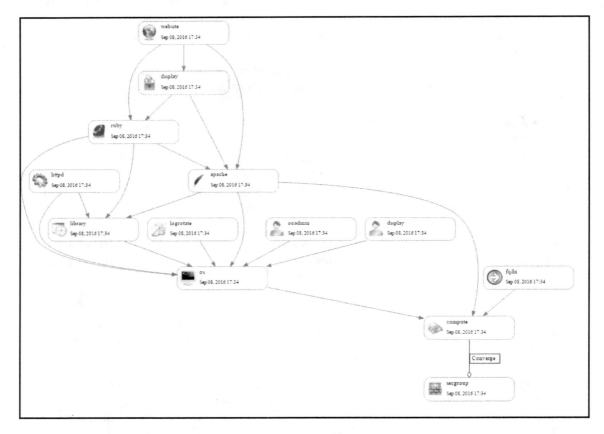

Design of Display assembly

Following are the platform-level variables that you will want to customize:

- **terms-of-service-url**: Change this to your terms of service URL, if you have one. It is actually a good idea to go into the OneOps code and actually edit the OneOps code to change the terms of service to reflect your own company's terms and conditions.

- **support-email**: This is the e-mail ID for your support group. If a different group is responsible for the upkeep of your OneOps instance, change this ID to reflect the e-mail ID of that group. That way all OneOps related emails can go to that email ID.

- **asset-url**: URL to an asset management system, in case you have one.

- **feedback-url**: URL to a feedback or metric gathering system on tickets and changes, if you have one.

- **help-url**: URL to your help site, wiki or knowledge-base.

- **news-url**: URL to any news site, if you have one.

- **privacy-policy-url**: URL to your company's privacy policy can go here.

- **report-problem-url**: URL to a form or other methods that users can use to report problems with the OneOps system, deployments, applications, and so on.

- **support-chat-url**: If your company uses any internal or external chat mechanisms, then the URL to that chat can go here. Chat support is more real-time and a better option for users than e-mail and more users prefer it to e-mail, forms, or other types of support.

Tomcat applications

After Display, OneOps installs a bunch of applications on Tomcat. Daq, sensor, antenna, transmitter, opamp, transistor, adapter and controller are all Java web applications that run on Tomcat. Although all applications have a different purpose, they all have a similar installation footprint.

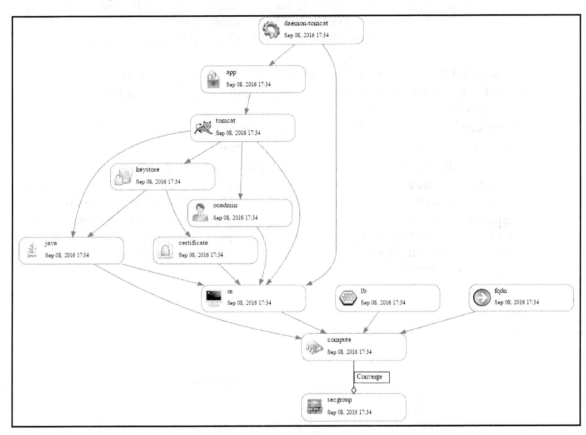

Tomcat is installed on top of an OS instance, along with a keystore and a certificate. The installer also installs the latest Java. The app itself runs on top of Tomcat. Tomcat runs as a daemon. The whole setup runs behind a load balancer, which balances the incoming requests in a round robin fashion. This is the one parameter that users might want to tune based on incoming load and usability.

- **Daq: Data Acquisition (Daq)** server provides a bunch of REST APIs to acquire data from collectors and insert them into Cassandra to be later used for graphing and aggregation. Collectors are small pieces of software installed on each and every instance that OneOps spins out. This piece of software gets installed during the compute phase of an instance spin up. Daq connects only to daqdb.

- **Sensor**: It consumes data from OneOps perf events. It generates events and API according to configured thresholds to determine the health of various CI and figure out their history. Sensor connects to opsdb, wire, opsmq, and cmsdb.

- **Antenna**: It is used for persisting and sending notifications to configured notification sinks. It is used internally from OpAmp and Controller to keep track on, inform and act upon events related to deployments. Antenna connects to wire and cmsdb.

- **Controller**: It is an Activiti-based workflow engine that is responsible for distributing work orders and action orders. As we saw before, any change to a CI that occurs in OneOps generates a work order or an action order depending on the situation. If a CI needs to be created, modified, or destroyed, a work order is generated by OneOps. However, if no material change is occurring to a CI and only updating or restarts are required, then action orders are generated. Various actions, such as deployments, uninstalls, restarts, autoscaling, autorepairs, and autoreplacements generate work orders and action orders depending on the appropriate situation. It is controller's job to generate and distribute the appropriate work orders and action orders to their actual destinations, which are usually various inductors. Controller connects to searchdb, activitidb, wire, and cmsdb.

- **Transmitter**: It is a webapps that takes changes from CMS and posts them to the messaging bus for all the subscribers to pick up. Transmitter connects directly to the wire and cmsdb.

- **Opamp**: It is a webapp that process operations events for change items such as unhealthy items and decides appropriate actions for those events. The events are picked up from the wire, where they are put by various other apps. Opamp connects directly to wire and cmsdb.

- **Transistor**: It is the core web application that aids in the creation of designs and deployment plans. It is also responsible for comparing what is deployed and what is supposed to be deployed according to the defined packs, user's changes made in configuration in design or transistor. Transistor also takes care of commits to the design and design history that is displayed in the web frontend. Transistor connects directory to cmsdb.
- **Adapter**: It is a web application that exposes a set of REST API to perform CRUD operations on CMSDB. It is primarily used from display and from the knife command line plugin to make changes to CIs in CMDB. Changes can be made to models, assemblies, environments, and so on. Adapter connects directly to cmsdb.

There are also a few interesting things to note about all web application installations. Tomcat gets installed in `/opt/tomcat7` directory and the webapps are installed in the `/opt/tomcat7/webapps` directory. OneOps also executes a few commands before Tomcat is shutdown and after Tomcat is started. You can find these commands if you click on Tomcat in any of these platforms, under the **Advanced** section.

Before Tomcat is shutdown, OneOps runs a clean shutdown on its ECV. Remember, ECV is used to monitor the health of Tomcat. The load balancer also uses the ECV URL to monitor the health of the Tomcat instance and uses it's results to take appropriate actions on Tomcat and the instance that it runs on. After Tomcat is started, OneOps runs a script in a loop to ensure that the ECV URL is up and running appropriately to ensure that Tomcat came up cleanly and is serving the expected application.

```
node.set["oneops"] = {

        :home => "/usr/local/oneops",
      :install_dir => "/usr/local/oneops"
    }
    node.set["tomcat"] = {
      :webapp_dir => "/opt/tomcat7/webapps"
    }
    tomcat_user = "tomcat"

    execute "rm -f /usr/local/oneops/dist"

    link "/usr/local/oneops/dist" do
       to "/opt/oneops/artifact/releases/$OO_LOCAL{version}/oneops/dist"
    end

    # war cleanup and deploy
    ["$OO_LOCAL{deploycontext}"].each do |war|

      execute "#{war} war clean" do
         command "rm -fr #{node[:tomcat][:webapp_dir]}/#{war}*"
      end
      execute "#{war} war deploy" do
         command "cp #{node[:oneops][:home]}/dist/#{war}*.war #{node[:tomcat][:webapp_dir]}"
      end
    end

    service "tomcat7" do
      action :restart
    end
#End of restart
```

As seen previously, every time Tomcat is restarted, the appropriate war is also deployed again.

Cassandra databases

OneOps uses two Cassandra databases in the backend. One is Ops DB and the second is DAQ DB. Of the two Ops, DB has a much simpler design, as it receives and stores data from Sensor.

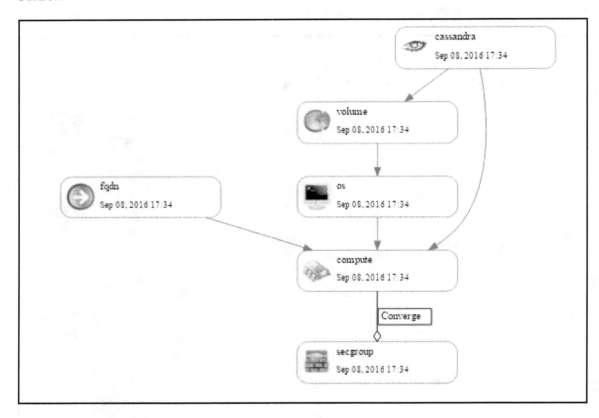

It is a simple Cassandra deployment with no log rotation, Logstash or backup configured. It merely acts as a place for messages to be dumped for later retrieval. The second Cassandra installation, daqdb, is a bit more complicated.

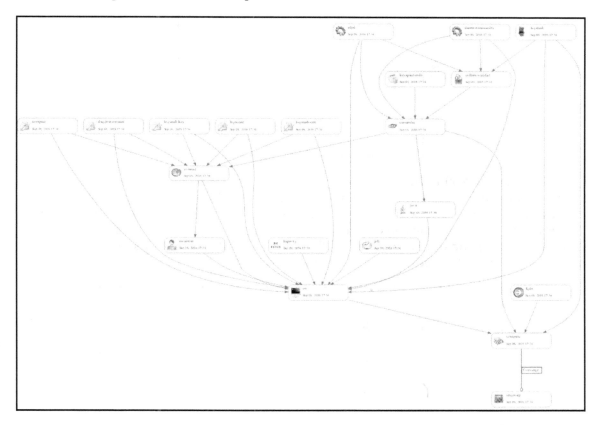

Design of daqdb assembly

Opsdb is deployed as a standalone Cassandra database. However daqdb is deployed as a Cassandra cluster. By default, the cluster is called **TestCluster**, however, you can change the name of the cluster if you want. OneOps also installs a collector artifact on each node of a Cassandra cluster. Each node of a Cassandra cluster also gets a ntp daemon installation to synchronize timestamps, since Cassandra depend upon accurate timestamps to synchronize data across nodes. Cassandra itself gets installed as a daemon.

OneOps installs an init script that makes each node join the cluster when it comes up. OneOps also implements log rotations via the log-rotate platform available internally. You can tune the parameter to retain fewer or more logs as necessary.

```
/opt/oneops/log/*.log
{
  copytruncate
  compress
  size 10M
  rotate 1
  prerotate rm -fr /opt/oneops/log/*.gz
  endscript
}
```

In front of the whole cluster, an HAProxy is deployed to load balance the nodes so that it can add nodes and remove unhealthy nodes as necessary. Also, on every node, OneOps creates a compaction script which runs compactions on the whole Cassandra namespace. This is a very disk space intensive operation. OneOps creates a job to run this operation. By default, this job is run once a week, every Friday at 2:40 PM. You can tune the frequency and timing of this job by editing the platform called **job**.

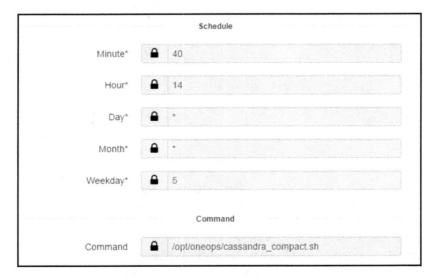

On Cassandra, a keyspace is created called **mdb**. Lastly, OneOps installs Logstash to pump log messages into the collector, which can in turn dump messages into Cassandra.

Postgres databases

OneOps has five postgres databases at the backend called **activitidb**, **displaydb**, **wiredb**, **searchmqdb**, and **cmsdb**. Each database store data about a different component of OneOps. Out of the four, activitidb, displaydb, searchmqdb and wiredb are simple installations, whereas cmsdb is a bit more of a complex installation.

Displaydb is used to store data about the frontend. It gets installed on a medium-sized instance and is not expected to grow much. It holds pretty much static data and gets populated at the time of install, like most Ruby on Rails applications do via migrations.

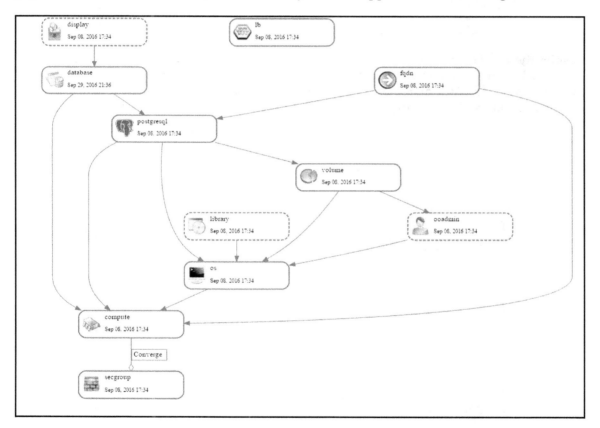

The only difference between displaydb, wiredb and activitidb install is, on displaydb instance, some extra libraries get installed which help the Rails to connect to postgres and to render graphs and perform other tasks.

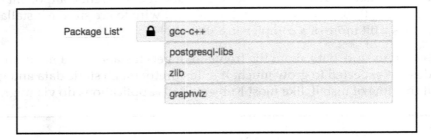

Besides these, all four database installations, that is displaydb, wiredb, searchmqdb, and activitdb look the same. In all three of the database installation, a load balancer is provided but not connected. You can either safely take it out or connect it if you are expecting load and want instances to be spun out when the load increases.

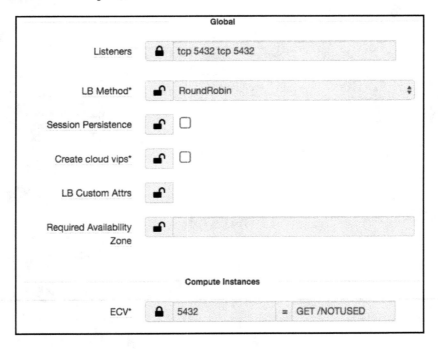

Cmsdb is a very important database. Hence, it's installation and design is a bit more complex than the other postgres databases. It has a lot more components, including initializations, snapshots, backups, and such.

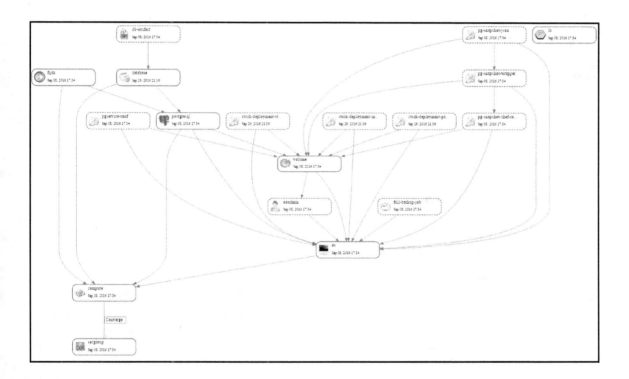

OneOps installs cmsdb on a large instance. The database instance itself is called **kloopzdb**. Every time the instance is installed or restarted, OneOps installs the database package from the Nexus repository. It's important to install this package from Nexus every time the instance is restarted, as this package installs new CIs and packs that the OneOps team releases frequently.

```
# disable this on secondary clouds in transition

conf = { :home => '/usr/local/oneops' }
node.set["oneops"] = conf

directory "#{node[:oneops][:home]}" do
  recursive true
end

bash "cms db schema" do
  cwd node[:oneops][:home]
  code <<-EOH
    tar zxf $OO_LOCAL{install-dir}/current/cms-db-pkg/db.tar.gz --no-same-owner --no-same-permissions
    cd db
    ./autoinstall-db.sh $OO_LOCAL{cms-db-user} $OO_LOCAL{cms-db-pass} > autoinstall-db.log 2>&1
  EOH
end
```

This script is also run as part of upgrading the OneOps codebase, as we will see in a future chapter. Besides this, OneOps creates various jobs that facilitates other activities across the system. It has three jobs that show stats on stuck deployments, stuck deployments that are paused, and stuck deployments that are in progress. All three jobs report the stats to **Nagios**. Besides the jobs that query deployments, there is also a job that configures snapshot backups based on a chef recipe. The backup is configured based on a json config file called `pg.snapshot.json`, which is created at the time of deployment. This file is picked up and run by a shell script called `pg-snapshot-wrapper.sh` via `chef-solo` to take snapshot backups of the database.

The snapshots are then copied to the backup host configured in the global variable BACKUP-HOST and the local copy is deleted. OneOps also configures a job component called full-backup-job that runs every four hours by default. You can tune this number to suit your purpose.

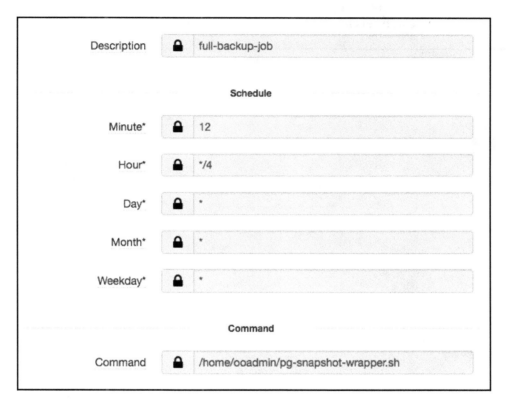

Lastly, as with the other database installation it provides a load balancer that is not really connected to the database. You can, however, choose to connect it if you think your database will incur a high load.

Messaging queues

OneOps uses activemq messaging for its message queue needs. Specifically, it uses three messaging servers on the backend. Again, just like the databases, the design of all three looks pretty much the same except for differences in configurations. Searchmq is a queue used by the elastic search service. If defines a queue called `search.stream`.

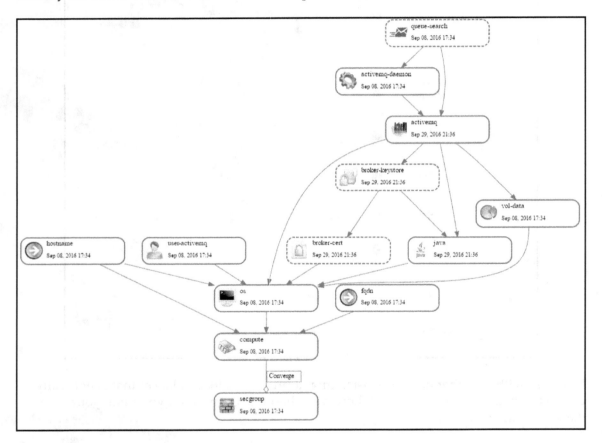

You have to change a few local variables here for this service to function properly. The variables that you will want to change are:

- `Amqpass`: The password set for ActiveMQ queues
- `Adminpass`: Administrator password for ActiveMQ
- `Broker-cert-pass`: Password for broker certificates used to encrypt data in the queue

OpsMQ is a very standard installation and design and there is no customization required. Wire is the central nervous system of OneOps, and much of the data flows through it. Before proceeding, some of the variables that you will want to change in wire are as follows:

- `Adminpass`: Administrator password for ActiveMQ
- `Broker-cert-pass`: Password for broker certificates, used to encrypt data in the queue

The design of wire is also a bit more complicated than the other queues. It also installs a host of other components compared to the other queues. To begin with, it installs the latest version of `oneops-amq-plugin` on top of the OS.

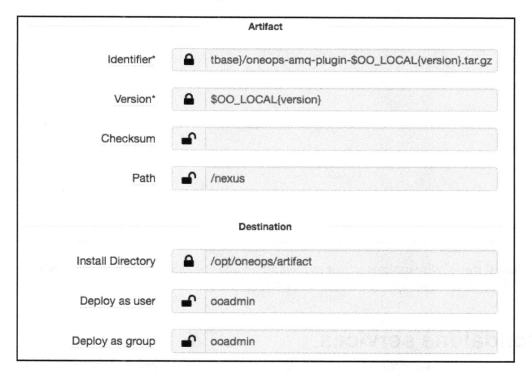

OneOps also creates five queues called `controller.response`, `search.stream`, `sensor-mgmt`, `CONTROLLER-WO`, and `NOTIFICATIONS`, and one topic called `CSM.ALL`.

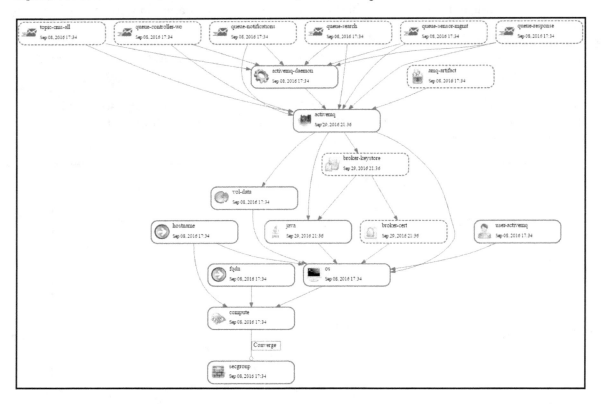

Besides all these, wire assigns a host name and an alias of kloopsmq to the instance on which it runs, so other apps can refer to it by that name.

Standalone services

Besides all of these services, OneOps also deploys a few standalone services that are not connected to the main battery of servers but do aid in overall operation of OneOps. One platform is called **eslog**, which deals with the elastic search logs. It is a standard elastic search deployment, which processes all the output from Logstash and inputs it into elastic search.

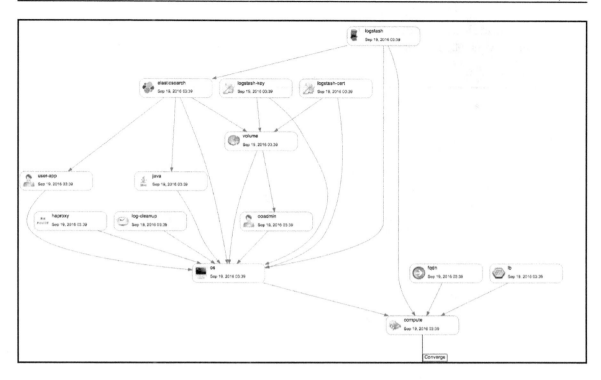

This platform collects all logs from Logstash and pumps them into elastic search. At the time of writing, a Kibana frontend is missing from this install but one can be easily added to enhance this install and make it more useful to sort to the logs, create useful dashboards, and dig out metrics. The same design also has the job of cleaning out logs every hour. It deletes logs that are older than an hour.

The second standalone platform is simply called **batch** and is a bit more complicated. True to its name, it runs a bunch of batch jobs to maintain the sanity of the OneOps system as a whole.

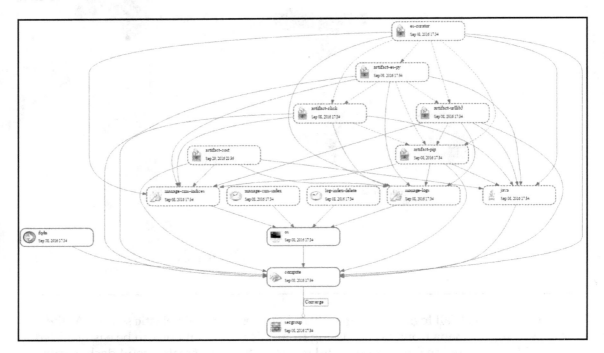

The first thing the platform does is to install a few dependencies, especially, in this case, some Python packages. Specifically, OneOps installs some dependencies, such as es-curator, es-py, urllib3, click, pip, and cost. Once done, it creates a few jobs across the cloud to manage the elastic search indices and logs across the whole cloud, namely manage-cms-indices, manage-logs, manage-cms-index, and log-index-delete.

All the jobs are based on maintenance scripts like the one preceding.

```
#!/bin/bash

source /etc/profile.d/oneops.sh
cloud_status=`printenv ONEOPS_CLOUD_ADMINSTATUS`

echo "cloud_status=$cloud_status"
if [ $cloud_status != "primary" ]; then
  echo "skipping because cloud status is secondary"
  exit
fi

curator --host es delete indices --older-than $OO_LOCAL{log_delete_days} --time-unit days --timestring '%Y.
curator --host es close indices --older-than $OO_LOCAL{log_close_days} --time-unit days --timestring '%Y.%m
```

After all the configuration is done and you have a good understanding of all the servers involved, you are finally ready to push the install button. As mentioned in the previous chapter, click on transition and create an appropriate environment for your assembly. Once you have created an environment design, pull should take a minute or so since this is a huge design. You are now ready to commit and do an enterprise deployment of OneOps. This is the last chance to review and make any changes to the design. If you are satisfied and ready, click on **Commit and Deploy** button. You will be given the option to restrict your deployment to only a few platforms or all of them. For the first deployment, you should select all of them and click **OK**.

At this point, two things can happen: either OneOps will generate a very big deployment plan for you, or you will get an error and OneOps will fail to generate a deployment plan for you. If you are getting an error, then you will have to work through the errors till all of them are resolved before the installation can proceed. The most common errors that you may face at this point are some variables that your forgot to change, illegal values in the variables, your Nexus repository is inaccessible, your other sources such as Python scripts or the Internet or other places are not accessible. You may also want to check your authentication, authorization, and accessibility. If all else fails, you may want to reach out to the OneOps team on their slack channel for help. You may also find me on the channel frequently. After you have worked through all the errors, you will find the OneOps has generated a big deployment plan for you. If you click on **Deploy**, OneOps will deploy the whole enterprise system for you. Since the original OneOps that you used to deploy the enterprise OneOps was also in the cloud, you can now manage the enterprise OneOps via the standalone OneOps. Should you want to deploy a redundant OneOps system, you can do so now either via your standalone OneOps or via the enterprise OneOps.

Summary

In this chapter, we saw how to bootstrap a standalone OneOps system in the cloud using the master build and then use that to install OneOps at an enterprise-level. An enterprise-level OneOps installation has much more standalone components compared to a single install. An enterprise-level install can also handle the loads and demands of a truly global organization with vast number of users, change items, packs, platforms, clouds, and deployments. A proper enterprise install can usher an organization from monolithic, spaced-out installs to rapid, self-service deployments. In the next chapter, we will see some practical deployment scenarios and how to build an assembly from scratch.

5
Practical Deployment Scenario

In the previous chapter, you saw how to install OneOps in an enterprise environment. While every enterprise has different needs, it gave good guidelines about how to install and scale a OneOps installation. In this chapter, we will look at a sample real-life application and take it through various phases of design, deployment, and maintenance. This chapter is less about the application and more about exploring all the features of OneOps that the application leverages. So, let's get right into it.

Deploying a load-balanced website with Apache HTTPD, Tomcat, and MySQL

Let's consider a typical Java-based web application. In our web-based application, we will have three tiers. The first tier will be the Apache HTTP Server, which will serve static pages and will pass on dynamic requests to an underlying Tomcat server. The Tomcat server will, in turn, communicate with a database server. The database server will be a MySQL server. This is by no means a perfect design and leaves a lot of scope for improvement, but it should serve our purpose of demonstrating the various features of OneOps for designing, promoting, and managing an assembly. Now, assuming you have a working instance of OneOps, log in with your username and password and click on **New Assembly**. Let's call our assembly **JavaApp**. Provide an appropriate owner e-mail address and click **Save**.

At this point, we will start adding platforms to our assembly. As mentioned before, our assembly will have three platforms.

Just to refresh your memory, roughly translated, an assembly contains all the instructions necessary to deploy an application, including the infrastructure required, such as the servers, containers, and so on; the platforms, on the other hand, are installable pieces of software or services that can be added or attached to the assembly.

To begin with, we will add Apache HTTP Server. The steps should be familiar and very similar to what we did in Chapter 3, *OneOps Application Life Cycle*. Let's start by adding a platform and calling it **WebServer**. In **Pack Source**, select **oneops**, and in **Pack Name**, select **Apache** and click **Save**:

You should see an assembly added that is very similar to the one added in Chapter 3, *OneOps Application Life Cycle*. You can see the website sits on top of the Apache web server, which itself sits on top of the OS, which in turn sits on top of the compute instance. The compute instance maps to an fqdn, and access to this is controlled via a security group. Now, before we move on, let's tweak a few options on our web server. Click on **Apache**, and you should see **Configuration Attributes**. Click on **Edit**. You should be able to edit several of the configuration attributes for Apache. Most of these configurations will go directly into Apache's configuration:

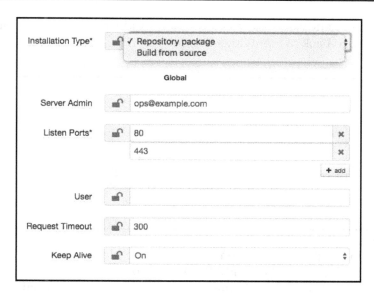

As you can see, you can either install a binary from a package, or else you can compile from source. You can also change the server admin e-mail address to something sane. You can also change the ports that the web server will listen to, and other options, such as request timeout, and so on. You should also consider disabling some options, such as TLSv1, which is generally insecure, and PHP info index, which can give out information on your installed PHP modules, thus making your site less secure:

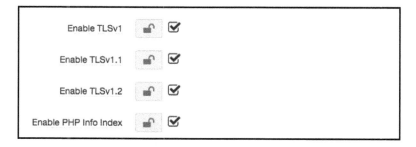

Once all your configurations are done, click on **Save**. At this point, you should go ahead and commit your changes. If you click on **design** on the left-hand side, you should see a **status** area in the middle of the screen that will give you the option to **Review**, **Discard**, or **Commit** your changes so far. **Review** allows you to review all the changes you have made to your assembly since your last commit, whereas Discard will allow you to abandon those changes. It is recommended that you frequently commit all your changes so OneOps can keep track of all your changes to an assembly.

This feature comes in handy, as your assembly design gets more complex and, sometimes, you feel the need to go back to a previous design.

So far, we have dealt with assemblies that have only one platform. We are now ready to add the next platform. Let's go ahead and add the Tomcat platform. We will call this platform **Webapp**. Make sure you select **link to the platform Web server**. This will create a dependency between the Apache web server and Tomcat.

Before we continue, we can tune some configuration, as we did for the web server. Click on **Webapp** and you should see a diagram showing the various components of the webapp, as well as the dependencies between them. The same components are also shown on the right-hand side:

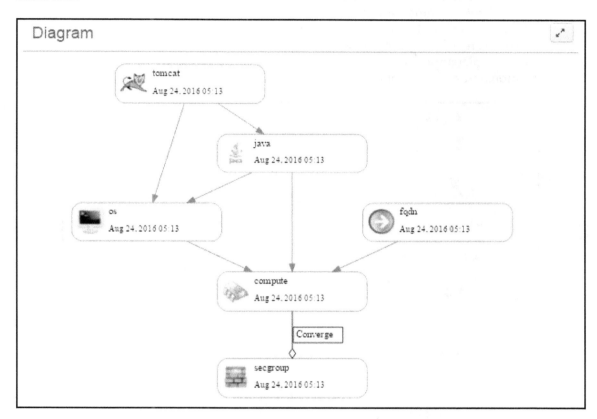

Click on **tomcat**, the yellow Tomcat image in the diagram, or you can scroll on the right-hand side and click on **Tomcat**. On the next page, click on **Edit** at the top. You should see various options that you can tune. This gives you a general idea of the amount of optimization that OneOps allows you to do for each application that you deploy. Along the top, in the **Global** section, you can choose whether you want to install Tomcat from the binary tarball or from the repository package. It also allows you to change the installation directory. You also have a choice of mirror sites, with the option of adding your own mirrors, should you desire to. You can also choose the install and build version and the webapps directory.

If you are familiar with Tomcat configuration, you will recognize the next section, the Server section, as the main Tomcat configuration. You can customize your Tomcat configurations in this section. Using any values you put here, OneOps will generate a custom configuration file for your Tomcat instance. If you scale up your Tomcat install, each install will get the same configuration. You can set a user and a group for your Tomcat install or leave it blank to default to the OS-specific user and group (Tomcat, in most instances). You can also set other values, such as HTTP port, SSL port, server port, and so on. For a brief explanation tooltip of any configuration, hover your mouse over the name of a configuration and a small explanation of the configuration will pop up.

	Server	
User		
Group		
Sets the protocol to handle incoming traffic for Connector*	HTTP/1.1	▾
Enable HTTP Connector	☑	
Additional attributes needed for connector config.*	connectionTimeout **=** 20000	✕
	maxKeepAliveReques **=** 100	✕
		+ add
HTTP Port*	8080	
SSL Port*	8443	
Server port*	8005	
AJP port*	8009	

In general, OneOps allows you to customize the configuration of software before you install it, and that configuration is carried over to all the instances that you scale. For example, had we chosen **ActiveMQ** as a platform component in our assembly design, we would have gotten options to customize it, as shown in the following screenshot:

	ActiveMQ	
Installation directory	🔓 /opt	
Version*	🔓 5.13.0	
Transport Connectors*	🔓 nio	= nio://0.0.0.0:61616
Log file Size (MB)	🔓 5	
Log file path	🔓 /var/log/activemq	
Maximum Connections	🔓 1000	
Environment Variables	🔓	

We can now go ahead and add our final platform, which is the database. Click on **Add Platform** and choose**MySQL** from the databases available. Under Links, be sure to select **Webapp**, since our Tomcat will be talking to the MySQL database; however, our web server does not need a direct connection to the database. Then click on **Save**.

As before, let's change a few database settings before we go ahead. As with all the other platform designs, you should see the following design for MySQL:

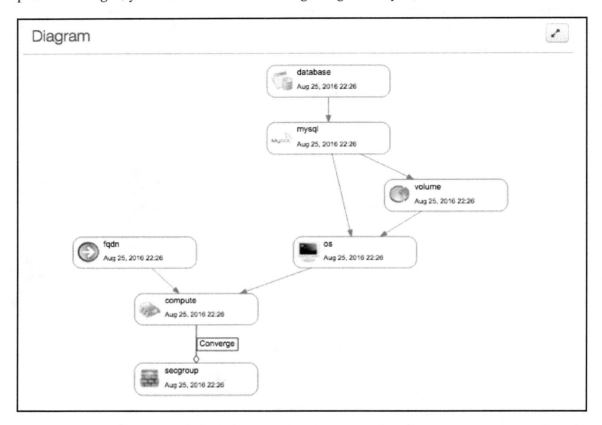

From here, you should be able to tune the settings for the whole MySQL install. If you click on the **mysql** icon, you will be taken to a screen where you can select the specific version to install, the root password, the data directory, and the listening port, among other things.

Note that, if you change the listening port to something other than the default here, you will also have to update the security group with the corresponding port. This is not done automatically for you.

Click on **Save** and then database under the design link on the left-hand navigation bar to be taken back to the screen with the diagram. Now click on the icon that says **database**. Here, you can change the name of the instance, the default user, and the password used to log into the instance.

Now, before we can install the final component, which is the load balancer, let's test our design so far. We are doing a test deployment at this point because what we have forms our base architecture. We would want to discover any flaws in it at this point. Any errors in it would get compounded later. So far, we have a web server, which connects to an application server, which connects to a database. Let's commit all the changes and click on **deploy**.

Deployment plan

If everything deploys correctly, we actually have a very useless deployment on our hands. Sure, we can connect to port 80 of the web server, the default web page loads, we can connect to port 8080 of the webapp, and the default page of Tomcat loads, but that was not our intention at all. So let's make it a bit more functional and deploy an actual webapp and then have Apache redirect an actual URL to Tomcat.

To deploy a webapp to Tomcat, we can use several methods. Click on **Tomcat** and then **design**. On the right-hand side, you will see several options available that can be utilized to deploy a webapp. You can use artifact to download a WAR file from a repository such as Nexus and install it on the Tomcat server. You can use the **download** option to download it from a URL. You can use the **file** option to execute a custom script to do a build and copy the war file over from a custom location. The target directory will always be `/opt/tomcat7/webapps`. For this demo, I am using the sample war file provided by Tomcat 7, which can be found at
`https://tomcat.apache.org/tomcat-7.0-doc/appdev/sample/sample.war`.

Once your webapp is downloaded, you can go to your Tomcat installation sample directory and see that that the sample webapp is successfully deployed, as shown here:

Sample "Hello, World" Application

This is the home page for a sample application used to illustrate the source directory organization of a web application utilizing the principles outlined in the Application Developer's Guide.

To prove that they work, you can execute either of the following links:

- To a JSP page.
- To a servlet.

However, you can see that we still have to go to the Tomcat server port `8080` and the `/sample` directory to access the webapp. Let's see if we can fix that and access it by redirecting the requests from our Apache web server.

If, at any point, things are not working out as planned, see the end of this chapter for common deployment errors and tips and tricks to troubleshoot them.

First, we need to enable `mod_proxy` on the Apache web server. Click on **JavaApp** and then**design**. Then click on **web server platform**. In the diagram in the middle of the screen, find the **Apache** icon and then click on it. Click on **Edit** on the top, then scroll down to see all the modules that have already been enabled. Click **add** at the bottom and add `mod_proxy` to enable `mod_proxy`:

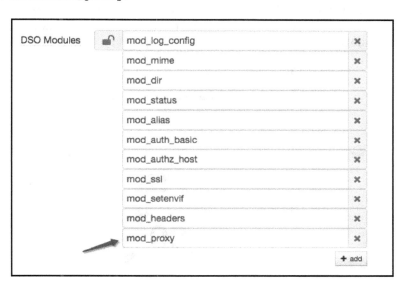

Once `mod_proxy` is added, scroll down to add the configuration that will map `/sample` on the web server to the `/sample` on the webapp server. Scroll down to where you see the custom configuration and add the configuration you can see in the following screenshot. **ProxyPass** and **ProxyPassReverse** are Apache configuration directives used to map a local URL to a specified remote URL. Apart from serving static pages, this will effectively turn your Apache server into a gateway server and cause it to pass certain requests to backend servers. Be sure to replace the server and domain names with the corresponding server and domain names for your webapp:

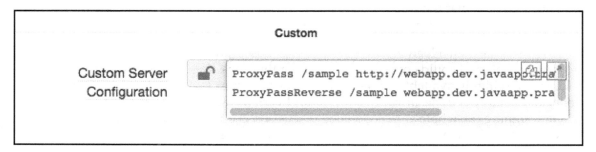

Click on **Save** and then commit your changes. You can then go to transition and deploy your changes. Once your changes are deployed, you may have to go to **Operations** and restart**Apache** server. To do so, click on **Operations** and then select **top of operations**. From the right-hand side, select the **platform**, in this case, web server. From the components on the right-hand side, select **Apache**, and you should see the deployed components. Click on the component, which is usually Apache followed by a 5-digit number, followed by a single digit. On the right-hand side, you will see actions to execute. If you click on that, one of the actions will be to restart Apache:

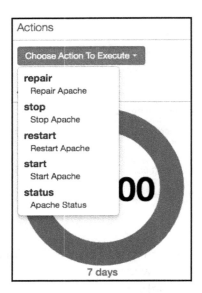

Choose **restart** and wait for a positive response. You can also see the logs for the sequence of events it follows to do the actual restart. Once the restart is done, if you follow the URL to your web server and `/sample` directory, you should see the same screen that you saw when you went to `/sample` on the Tomcat server. Now, there is just one small loop hole that exists. Port `8080` is still accessible to the world on the Tomcat server. There is absolutely no need for that now that the web server is forwarding all traffic to Tomcat. This can be easily fixed by modifying the security rules, but I will let you figure that out.

Finally, we can install a load balancer for our web-based Java application. Load balancing is a complex topic and could cover a large chunk of this book. Designing a properly load-balanced and highly available application is a very complex task. Load balancing can be done, and usually is done, at various levels, and various factors are taken into consideration when designing the whole app. A detailed discussion is outside of the scope of this book. We can add load balancing to our deployment in two ways.

One way is to use the use the load balancers provided by the cloud vendors, and the second is to add our own load balancer by adding a platform called **HAProxy**. Both approaches have their pros and cons. HAProxy is more platform-agnostic and will make your assembly work the same no matter where you deploy, even on an internal cloud such as OpenStack. However, you will also have to do much of the configuration and make sure you handle the load properly. On the other hand, using the vendor-provided load balancer takes much of the guess-work out of the configuration and scaling. However, this also confines the deployment of your assembly to those particular vendors. To use the vendor-provided load balancer, your assembly should be deployed in redundant mode, under availability, under transition.

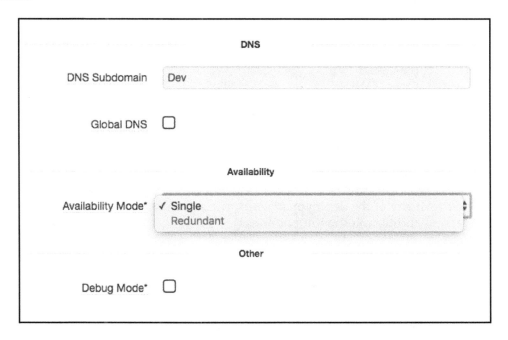

If you have selected redundant mode, then your assembly will already have the LB component. Click on **transition** and then **web server**; on the right-hand side you should see the **LB component**. Click on the **LB component** to set the various options. Currently, the LB listens on ports 80 and 8080. Since we will be using the LB for our Apache web server, we will change port 8080 to 80. You can also choose between the two load balancing methods of round robin and the least connections. You can also choose session persistence if necessary. This means, if one of your backend servers establishes a session with a client, all subsequent requests will go to the same server.

And you can also set any availability zones to force your load balancer to work in a particular availability zone, if necessary:

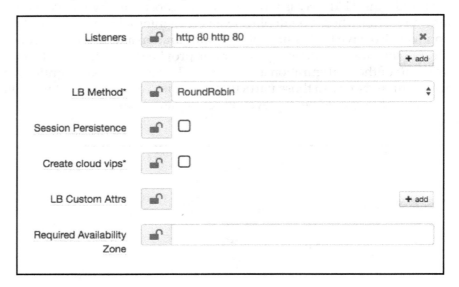

At this point, your assembly should be good enough to be deployed. Go ahead and commit all the changes. Then, transition to your favorite cloud and deploy the assembly. If you are having trouble with any of the deployment steps, check the end of this chapter for common deployment errors and troubleshooting options.

Adding SSL to your HTTPD

So far, the communication between our client and Apache has not been encrypted. SSL is the standard used for end to end encryption on the Web. There are two ways you can add SSL to your assembly here. One is, you can add SSL to your Apache web server so that the traffic between your client and the web server is encrypted. Apache then decrypts the traffic. In our case, Apache is serving the static pages, whereas the dynamic content is passed on to Tomcat. In this scenario, the traffic between Apache and Tomcat remains unencrypted. This reduces the load on Tomcat. However, this also assumes that the network connection between Tomcat and the web server is secure.

 Please note *how to secure the connection* is left to you and not mentioned in this book.

In the second scenario, the connections to Tomcat are passed on as is and are decrypted at the Tomcat end. This complicates things a bit because now we have to deal with two SSL certificates: one at the Apache and another at the Tomcat end. This also increases the load on Tomcat because it has to decrypt each request before it can process it. However, in this scenario, we do not have to worry about the security between Apache and Tomcat, although it is still a good idea to secure that part. In this case we will be looking at the first scenario and installing SSL on Apache. Either in transition or design, click on the website component. Ensure that you add port 443 as the **Listen Port**, as SSL listens on this port. Set **SSL** to **On**:

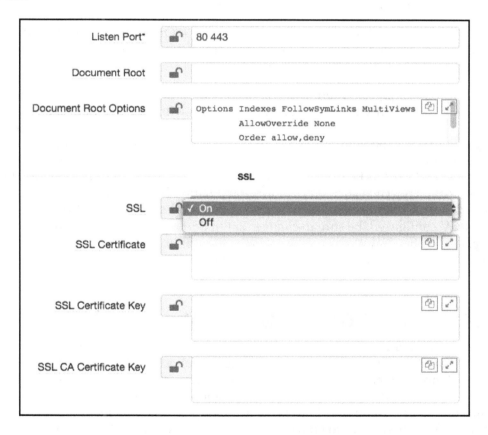

If you have bought a SSL certificate, you should have three files. Copy and paste the SSL certificate in the box that says **SSL Certificate**. You will want to copy and paste all the section that says **-BEGIN CERTIFICATE-** and ends with **-END CERTIFICATE-** . Secondly, you may have a CA certificate key, either in the same file or a different file in the same format. Copy and paste that in the SSL CA Certificate Key box. Lastly, unless you have a .key file, you will need to convert a .pem file to .key file and then copy and paste the contents into the SSL Certificate Key box. For this, you will need openssl installed. Run the following command to convert the file:

```
openssl rsa -in filename.pem -out filename.key
```

You will be asked for the passphrase for filename.pem. Once you provide the passphrase, you will have a decrypted filename.key. Copy and paste the contents of filename.key to SSL certificate.key.

There are a few other places where you will need to add these details to make your website work properly. Since our website is load-balanced, you will need to add a load balance component to the web server so the load balancer can properly decrypt the SSL traffic. In the design phase, click on **web server**. On the right-hand side, click on the + next to **lb-certificate**. You will see a screen asking pretty much the same details as previously. Enter all the certificate details as before and click on **Save**. Lastly, click on transition and then the desired environment. Then click on your assembly name. On the right-hand side, click on the load balancer. Under listener, remove port 80 and add **ssl_bridge 443 ssl_bridge 443**. If you have ECV configured, be sure to change that to port 443 too. Commit and deploy your assembly. Remember, any changes to Apache configuration do not take effect automatically. You will have to restart your web server manually by going to **Operations**.

Autoscaling your assembly

After your deployment steps are generated and your assembly is deployed, you have to be prepared to handle all kinds of load via your assembly. Fortunately, you chose to deploy via a load balancer, which does most of the work for you. You can configure the scaling up and down of your assembly in advance, so as to handle any anticipated load. It is also important that you set some smart limits on scaling up, so as not to incur any unnecessary costs in case your app decides to go rogue on you and blows the CPU limit due to a bug, rather than genuine load. You can configure your autoscaling options by either going to transition, under the assembly or going to the LB component, under transition.

Here, you can control the scaling of backend compute instances:

Component	% Deploy	Current	Min	Max	Step Up	Step Down
compute	100	2	2	10	1	1

By default, it deploys 100%, in this case two instances and maintains a minimum of two instances. However, it does not exceed a maximum of 10 instances. As the load increases, OneOps starts spinning new compute instances to handle the load. Since the **Step Up** value is **1**, it will spin one instance at a time. Similarly once the load decreases it will also kill instances one at a time since **Step Down** value is 1 to bring the minimum number of instances down to two. All of these numbers are tunable.

Adding autorepair and autoreplace

Autorepair and autoreplace can be added to your assembly to keep it healthy and running in the event of foreseen and unforeseen interruptions. Autorepair automatically tries to heal your instances that are marked as unhealthy by OneOps because they triggered some healthy violation or missed a heartbeat. Both autorepair and autoreplace are configured at platform level and after an assembly is deployed. Autorepair is attempted before autoreplace and the methods differ on a case-by-case basis. For example, for Apache web server autorepair might try to restart the service if it's not responding.

However, for a compute node, it might try to reboot it. Similarly for a disk node, there might not be an autorepair procedure at all. If autorepair does not resolve the issue with a platform, the instance is marked for autoreplace. Autoreplace is triggered when the instance remains unhealthy despite OneOps's best efforts. Once an instance is marked for autoreplace, it is replaced with a fresh instance of equivalent configuration and the old one is decommissioned:

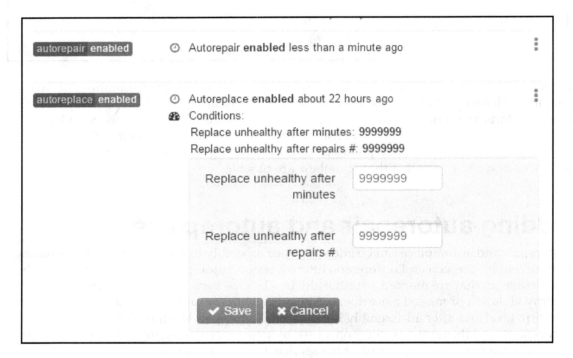

Both autorepair and autoreplace can be configured by going to **Operations** and clicking on the respective platform for an assembly. Go to the platform status area and click on three dots next to **Auto Repair**, to either enable or disable it. If you click on the three dots next to **Auto Replace** you can either **enable/disable** it or edit its settings. By default, the **Replace unhealthy after minutes** and **Replace unhealthy after repair** numbers are set to very large values. This means that, technically, autoreplace will never get triggered and OneOps will just try to autorepair the platform when a problem is encountered. To ensure autoreplace gets triggered after a set number of failed autorepair attempts, set the numbers to a sane value.

Deploying to multiple clouds

One of the hallmarks of OneOps is its ability to deploy the same assembly to multiple clouds. By definition, OneOps is multi-cloud management software. If you have multiple clouds defined in your OneOps installation, and it's highly recommended that you have multiple clouds, then you can deploy your assembly in parallel to both the clouds.

 Why deploy to multiple clouds ? There are several reasons you should consider doing this. The most common reason is to deploy to multiple geographic zones. When you deploy an application, you may want to configure it in such a way that clients in a particular part of the world are routed to the nearest datacenter. You may also want to deploy to different vendors to maintain redundancy, or for pricing reasons and, ultimately, choose a vendor that offers better pricing.

However, you have to take a few things into consideration before you deploy the assembly to multiple clouds. You will have to pick which cloud will be your primary and which one will be your secondary. You can also choose both to be primary clouds in case you want your solution to be a truly highly available solution. For true redundancy, you can choose one cloud to be primary and one to be secondary:

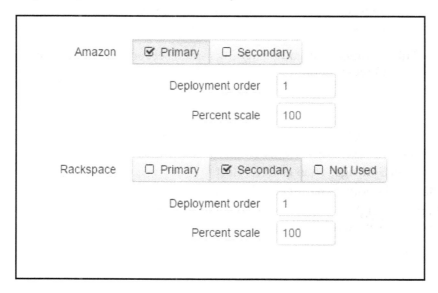

The important thing to note here is the deployment order. The even numbered deployment order gets preference over the odd numbered deployment order. The actual numbers themselves are meaningless, as such. Once you have chosen the appropriate setting from the transition phase, choose **Save** and then deploy your assembly. It should get deployed to multiple clouds.

Understanding and resolving common deployment errors

Errors and missteps are common in any project. OneOps offers very good feedback over most errors and methods of recovering from them. Below are some common pitfalls that you may face and how to recover from them.

Unable to get notifications of deployments and other events

By default, notifications are disabled in OneOps and have to be enabled manually in each assembly. Follow these steps to enable notifications for one or more of your assemblies:

 This assumes that your outgoing e-mail server is configured properly on your OneOps server.

1. Log in to the OneOps server with your username and password.
2. Click on the assembly that you want notifications for.
3. Click on **Settings**. Then click on **Edit**.
4. Make sure your e-mail ID is updated and accurate in the **Owner** field.
5. In the top-right hand corner, under **Email Notifications**, you will currently see **Ignoring** selected. Click on it and select **Watch**:

Once you have followed these directions, you will start receiving e-mail notifications when a deployment starts and finishes. You will also get e-mail notifications when some operations events happen on your assembly, such as an application restarting or some scaling of your compute instance.

Compute instance installation hangs

Sometimes, your compute installation will hang and time out. Usually, if you just retry the installation, the issue will resolve itself; however, if the issue does not resolve itself, there are a few steps you can try and troubleshoot to get your instance up and running. When a compute instance is provisioned, there are a series of steps that are followed by OneOps to get the compute instance up and running. As a first step, OneOps generates a pair of keys to log into the provisioned instance. Secondly, OneOps will generate a security group to control access to the compute instance. The minimum rule that OneOps will add to the security group will be the SSH port 22. However, in this instance, if you see the deployed security group in the cloud, in most instances, the security group will not be deployed properly and port 22 will be missing from it.

During deployment, OneOps goes into a loop for port 22 to be accessible for a certain amount of time and then times out. OneOps needs SSH to be active because it uses SSH to log in to the compute instance and install custom OneOps components to control and monitor the instances. You can quickly fix this while the deployment is in progress, provided you have access to the backend cloud:

- During the deployment, click on the **Security Group** that was created. This will take you to the **Security Groups Details** screen.
- Under the **Important Attributes**, note the security **Group ID** and the security **Group Name**.

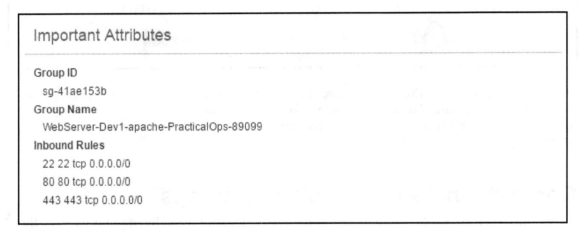

1. Log in to the backend cloud directly, for example, in this instance AWS.
2. Navigate to the **Security Group** and find it using the ID or the name.
3. Quickly edit it and add port 22.
4. Click on **Save**.

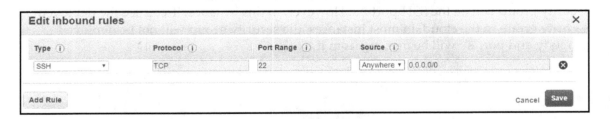

As soon as you do this, your compute installation should continue installation.

You want Ops team to approve deployments

By default, if you don't control access, anyone can do deployments via OneOps. This works out well in small shops where the hierarchy is flat and access control and not very tight. However, in an enterprise environment where you have a separate Ops team, you may want to define the Ops team differently, have each deployment to production vetted, and have a stamp of approval from an Ops person before the deployment can proceed. Follow these steps to add approvals to any cloud:

Make sure you are logged in as an admin for your organization. Click on the **Organization name** and then click on the small sliders in the top-right hand corner to edit the organization.

1. Click on **Teams** and **Add Team**.
2. Add a team name such as Ops or DevOps.
3. Make sure **Organization Scope** is checked.
4. Make sure **Support** is checked under **Cloud Permissions**.

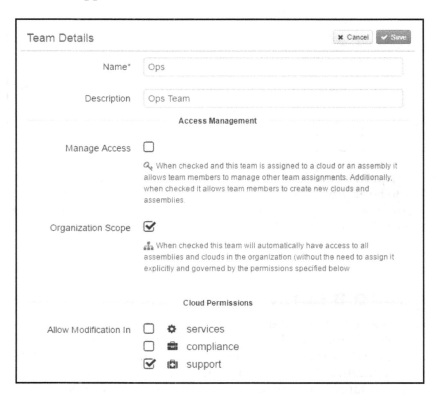

5. Once done, click on clouds on the left-hand side. Then click on the cloud where you would like to add the permissions.
6. Click on the **Support** tab. Click **Add Support**.
7. Give a name such as Ops or DevOps and a good description, such as **Ops needs to approve deployment**.
8. Make sure **Enable and Deployment Approval** are checked.
9. Click **Save**.

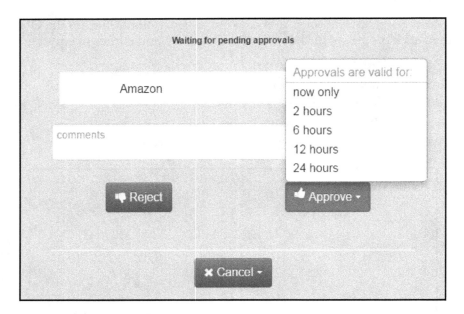

Now, when you request a new deployment to the cloud and a deployment plan is generated, it has to be approved by someone in the team, as shown in the preceding screenshot. Not only can you approve the deployment once, but you can make the approval stick for a predetermined time for subsequent deployments of the assembly for the same cloud.

Logging in to a compute instance

When you create an assembly, generally, you include all the definitions required to construct the assembly in the assembly itself. This includes the underlying infrastructure required to run your code, such as the compute instance and things such as DNS required to reference your application. Most of the time, it is recommended and good practice to treat your compute instance like a container or a black box and never log in to it.

However, there might be a time when you require direct access to a compute instance to troubleshoot your assembly, look up a log, or look up a configuration. Although this is not recommended, sometimes this is the quickest way to get something done:

 Be warned, if you make any changes to the compute instance and do not propagate this change back to your assembly, the next deployment will wipe out this change. This can cause configuration drift. Therefore, this approach to change is never recommended.

1. Either make sure you are operating from Linux, a Linux-like client, or you have OpenSSH installed.
2. If you don't have a SSH key, generate a SSH key by running the following command:

```
ssh-keygen -t rsa -C <your_email@company.com>
```

3. This will generate a new public and private key for you and save them in the default location of ~/.ssh.
4. Now click on your **Assembly**, and from the right-hand menu, **Add a user** component.
5. Choose an appropriate name for the user, hopefully the same as the one you used to generate the SSH key.
6. Choose a **home directory** and enable sudo access if you need system-wide access to troubleshoot things.
7. Click on the + next to authorized keys. Copy and paste the contents of your ~/.ssh/id_rsa.pub file.
8. If you have keys in multiple locations, such as laptop and desktop, add them all here. Then click on **Save**.

9. Now commit and deploy your assembly.

Once your assembly is successfully deployed, you can go to operations and find out the name of FQDN of your compute instance and simple SSH into it by issuing the following command:

```
ssh username@fqdn
```

You want to manage your assembly

After your assembly is deployed, you can manage its various components by going to the operations sections. OneOps offers very fine-grained control of all the components of your assembly. You can do everything, from viewing the logs to stopping and starting the instances, to initiating repairs from the operations section. For example, if you want to reboot an errant compute instance, follow these steps:

1. Click on your **Assembly** and then **Operations**.
2. Select the **environment** where you wish to initiate the reboot.
3. Select the **platform** where the instance is located.

4. Select the **instance** from the right-hand side and then select the **deployed instance**.

5. You can see the overall health and status of the instance. In the top right-hand corner you will see a big, green button, which will allow you to perform various actions on this instance.

6. Choose an appropriate action:

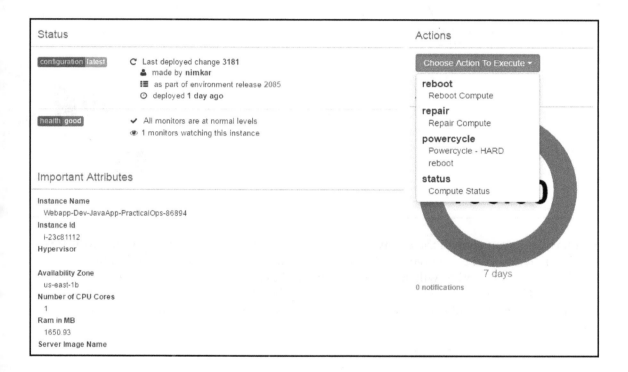

You can perform similar actions on any of the other platforms. For example, on Apache web server you can perform actions such as stop, start, and restart the web server instead of restarting the whole instance:

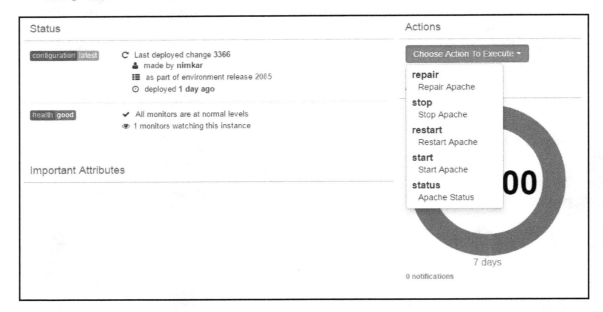

Similarly, you can control the behavior of all the components. If you click on the **Monitors** tab, it will show you the active monitors and the graph of currently collected data. Similarly, the notification will show you the overall availability and health trends of the assembly. This can come in handy while planning the scaling factor of your assembly. Lastly, the **Logs** tab will show you the logs for the component, which are sortable and searchable.

Best practices

Here are a few best practices to follow when using OneOps. Lots of these are suggested by the OneOps team in their official documentation. I have tried to provide justification for some of them where possible:

- Follow a set naming convention for assembly names. OneOps sets some rules as to how you can name an assembly, such as no spaces. Also remember that your assembly name will become part of your FQDN after deployment, so choose a good assembly name.

- Always add owner's e-mail ID to your assembly and enable watching. Be responsible for your own deployments. That's what DevOps is all about!
- Be cognizant of the default values and tune them accordingly. Sometimes, the defaults will trip you up.
- Choose good and descriptive platform names. A good suggestion is name them according to the platform you are adding, that is, if you are adding Postgres, then call it Postgres or Postgres-middleware.
- Do not make changes directly to an instance, even if you can. You will cause configuration drift. Always change your assembly and deploy again.
- Choose sane and descriptive environment names such as QA, PPE, and Prod. A, B, and C are not good names.
- Always publish CNAME to your application and not the address of the underlying instance. The underlying instance might get replaced.
- Always have autorepair enabled. If you must have autoreplace enabled, then choose good values for autorepair before autoreplace is attempted.
- Follow the principle of least privileges. This maintains security. Only give enough access to anyone for them to complete their task. Avoid excess. Create logical teams to segregate access.
- Enable approvals by Ops team for deployments to sensitive systems in productions to maintain their stability.
- Keep a frequent eye on the logs, usage, metrics, and thresholds. This includes e-mails that OneOps will send you.
- Clean up after yourself and undeploy unused apps.

Summary

In this chapter, we saw a real-world example of deploying an app that consisted of a web server that communicated with a webapp, that also had a database as a backend. Although we did deploy a sample application on the Tomcat that did not do much, the goal of the chapter was to demonstrate the various features of OneOps and how easy and powerful all of its features are to use. In the next chapter, we will see how to manage our OneOps instance from an administrator's point of view.

6
Managing Your OneOps

In the previous chapter, we saw how to create and deploy an application in a practical scenario. We also saw how to use features, such as scaling, autorepair, and autoreplace to manage our assembly once it was deployed. However, as DevOps, you will have to manage not only assemblies but the OneOps system itself. Depending on the size of the organization and the complexity of the deployments you handle, you may opt to choose either a single-server installation or an enterprise installation. Managing both kinds of systems and keeping them up to date require different kinds of steps. In this chapter, we will look at a few steps that will help you manage both kinds of installations.

Upgrading OneOps with minimal downtime

As mentioned earlier, you might be running a standalone instance of OneOps or an enterprise instance. For both types, you will have to use different strategies to update the OneOps code. In general, it is easier and more straightforward for updating a standalone instance rather than an enterprise instance. Your strategies to update and the branch or tag of code that you will use will also differ based on the kind of system that you have.

Updating a standalone OneOps installation

If you have a standalone installation, it's possible that you created it in one of several ways. You either installed it using **Vagrant**, as mentioned in Chapter 1, *Getting Started with OneOps,* or using the **Amazon Machine Images (AMI)** again, as mentioned again in Chapter 1, *Getting Started with OneOps*. It is also possible that you built your own installation on another cloud such as Google, Azure, or Rackspace as per the instructions in Chapter 4, *OneOps Enterprise Deployment*.

Irrespective of the way your instance of OneOps was created, the steps to upgrade it remain the same and are very simple. If you recall from `Chapter 1`, *Getting Started with OneOps*, and `Chapter 4`, *OneOps Enterprise Deployment*, when you set up OneOps, two scripts are run by the setup process, `oo-preqs.sh` and `oo_setup.sh`. Once an instance is set up, both these scripts are also copied to the `/home/oneops` directory on the server. Of these two scripts, `oo_setup.sh` can be used to update an OneOps standalone installation at any time:

```
Downloads — root@ip-172-31-52-21:/home/oneops — ssh -i OneOps.pem cen...
#!/bin/sh

export BUILD_BASE='/home/oneops/build'
export OO_HOME='/home/oneops'
export GITHUB_URL='https://github.com/oneops'

mkdir -p $BUILD_BASE

if [ -d "$BUILD_BASE/dev-tools" ]; then
  echo "doing git pull on dev-tools"
  cd "$BUILD_BASE/dev-tools"
  git pull
else
  echo "doing dev tools git clone"
  cd $BUILD_BASE
  git clone "$GITHUB_URL/dev-tools.git"
fi
sleep 2

cd $OO_HOME

cp $BUILD_BASE/dev-tools/setup-scripts/* .

"oo_setup.sh" 24L, 455C
```

You need an active Internet connection to upgrade OneOps.

You can see the list of releases in the OneOps git repository for any of the OneOps components. For example, releases for sensor can be seen at `https://github.com/oneops/sensor/releases`.

Release candidates have RC1 at the end, and stable releases have *STABLE* at the end. If you want to install a particular release, such as 16.09.29-RC1, then invoke the script and pass the release number as the argument. Passing `master` will build the master branch and will build and install the latest and greatest code. This is great to get all the latest features and bug fixes, but this will also make your installation susceptible to new bugs:

```
./oo_setup.sh master
```

Ensure that the script is invoked as root. Instead of running as `sudo`, it helps if you are logged in as root with:

```
sudo su -
```

The reason to run as root is because the script itself calls other scripts, as mentioned here, and installs a lot of software, so running as root helps. After the script is invoked, it will do a bunch of things to upgrade your OneOps.

First, it sets three variables:

- `OO_HOME`, which is set to `/home/oneops`
- `BUILD_BASE`, which is set to `/home/oneops/build`
- `GITHUB_URL`, which is set to `https://github.com/oneops`

All the builds will take place under `BUILD_BASE`.

Under `BUILD_BASE`, the script then checks whether `dev-tools` exists. If it does, it updates it to the latest code by doing `git pull` on it. If it does not, then it does a `git clone` and gets a latest copy from GitHub. The `dev-tools` repository has a set of tools for core OneOps developers. The most important of which are under `setupscripts sub directory`.

The script then copies all the scripts from under `setupscripts sub directory` to the `OO_HOME` directory. Once done, it invokes the `oneops_build.sh` script. If you passed a `build` tag to the `oo_setup.sh` script, that tag is passed on to the `oneops_build.sh` script as is.

The `oneops_build.sh` script is a control script so to speak. In turn, what it means is it will invoke a bunch of other scripts, which will shut down services, pull and build the OneOps code, install the built code, and then restart the services once done.

Most of the scripts that run henceforth set and export a few variables, namely OO_HOME, BUILD_BASE and GITHUB_URL. Another variable that is set is SEARCH_SITE whose value is always set to localhost.

The first thing the script does is to shut down Cassandra on the server to conserve memory on the server and reduce the load during the build, since the build itself is very memory- and CPU-intensive. It also marks the start time of the script. Next, it runs the install_build_srvr.sh script by passing the build tag that was passed to the original script. This is a very innovative script, which does a quick installation of Jenkins, installs various plugins to Jenkins, runs various jobs to do builds, monitors the jobs for either success or failure, and then shuts down Jenkins all in an automated fashion.

If you have your own Jenkins installation, I highly recommend that you read through this script as this will give you great ideas for your own automation of installation, monitoring, and controlling Jenkins.

As mentioned earlier, the install_build_srvr.sh script sets a bunch of variables first. It then clones the git repository named build-wf from BUILD_BASE if it does not already exist. If it does exist, it does git pull to update the code. Outside of a Docker container, the build-wf is the most compact Jenkins installation you will find. You can check it out at:

https://github.com/oneops/build-wf.

It consists of Rakefile to download and install Jenkins and its associated plugins, a config.xml that configures it, a plugins.txt that provides a list of plugins, and a jobs directory with all the associated jobs in it.

Rake is Ruby's equivalent of Make, Linux's favorite build tool. As such the Makefile equivalent in Ruby is Rakefile. A Rakefile can be used to build different Ruby systems. It can also be used to download, configure, and install other systems. As in this case, it is being used to download, configure, and install a temporary Jenkins installation.

If the script detects a Jenkins server that is already present and a build is already in progress, it cleanly attempts to shut down the existing Jenkins server. It then attempts to install the latest Jenkins jar using the following command:

```
rake install
```

Once the installation is done, a dist directory is created to store the resulting build packages. After setting the path to local Maven, the server is brought up using the following command:

```
rake server
```

If you did not specify what revision to build, the last stable build is used:

```
rake server

sleep 5

ref="$1"
if [[ -z $ref ]]; then
  ref=16.06.03-STABLE  ◄─────
fi

echo "submit build $ref"
curl -X POST http://localhost:3001/job/oo-all-oss/build --data token=TOKEN --dat
a-urlencode json="{'parameter': [{'name':'REF', 'value':'$ref'}, {'name':'VERSIO
N', 'value':'continuous'}, {'name':'TAG', 'value':'false'}, {'name':'PUSH_TAG',
'value':''}]}"

GREP_RETURN_CODE=0
[]
# Poll every thirty seconds until the build is finished
while [ $GREP_RETURN_CODE -eq 0 ]
do
    echo "waiting jenkins build job to complete"
    sleep 30
    # Grep will return 0 while the build is running:
```

The actual release revision itself is hardcoded in this script. Every time a stable release is made, this file is manually changed and the release version is updated and the file is checked in. After the server comes up, it is available at port 3001 if you are running on any cloud. If you are running a Vagrant setup, it will be mapped to port 3003. If you connect to one of these ports on your machines via your browser, you should be able to see your Jenkins in action:

The script calls the job `oo-all-oss` via `curl` using Jenkins `REST API`. `oo-all-oss` is a master job that in turn builds all of OneOps components, including the database components. Even the installation of Jenkins plugins is done via a Jenkins job named **Jenkins-plugin**. The script then goes into an infinite loop and keeps checking the job status till the jobs are done. Once all jobs are finished or if an error is encountered, the server is shut down using the following:

```
rake stop
```

Once the build completes, the Cassandra sever is started again. Once it starts the `Cassandra` service, the script starts deploying all the built artifacts. The first artifact to be deployed is the database artifact. For that, it runs the `init_db.sh` script. This script first creates the three main schemas, namely `kloopzapp`, `kloopzdb`, and `activitidb`. Because you are upgrading an existing installation, this script may very well give an error. Next, the script will run a bunch of database scripts that will create tables, partitions, functions, and other `ddl` statements. Again since you are upgrading, any errors here can be safely ignored.

Next to be installed is the display. The script backs up the current display from `/opt/oneops/app` to `/opt/oneops/~app` in case a rollback is needed. It then copies and untars the newly built package. Using `rake`, it detects if the Rails database is set up. If the database version is returned as 0, then the `rake db:setup` command is run to set up a brand new database. Otherwise, the `rake db:migrate` command is run to migrate and upgrade the database.

The next component to get installed is `amq`. This is done by calling the script `deploy_amq.sh`. The `amq` gets installed in the directory `/opt/activemq`. Before installation, the `activemq` service is stopped. The script then copies over the `amq-config` and `amqplugin-fat` jar. It also takes a backup of the old configuration and overwrites it with the new configuration. After that, the service is started again.

After AMQ, the script installs all `webapps` under **Tomcat**. Tomcat itself is installed under `/usr/local/tomcat7`, and all `webapps` gets installed under `/usr/local/tomcat7/webapps`. Before copying over all the `war` files, the `tomcat` service is stopped. The script also creates directories that the controller, publisher, and transmitter rely on for successful operation. Once the wars are copied, Tomcat service is started again. Tomcat, at this point, will automatically deploy the services.

After the web services are deployed, the script deploys the `search` service. Before deployment, the `search-consumer` service is stopped. The `search.jar` and the `startup` script is then copied to the `/opt/oneops-search` directory, and the `search-consumer` service is started again.

As a final step in deployment, the **OneOps Admin gem** is deployed. The OneOps Admin gem contains two commands that help administer OneOps from the backend. These commands are `inductor` and `circuit`. The script then either updates the circuit repository if it exists or clones it if it does not from `https://github.com/oneops/circuit-oneops-1` and installs it. After successfully installing the circuit, an inductor is created using the shared queue using the command later. This command is also a great reference for you should you wish to create your own inductors for testing. This will be covered in the later chapter:

```
inductor add --mqhost localhost
--dns on
--debug on
--daq_enabled true
--collector_domain localhost
--tunnel_metrics on
--perf_collector_cert /etc/pki/tls/logstash/certs/logstash-forwarder.crt
--ip_attribute public_ip
--queue shared
--mgmt_url http://localhost:9090
--logstash_cert_location /etc/pki/tls/logstash/certs/logstash-forwarder.crt
--logstash_hosts vagrant.oo.com:5000
--max_consumers 10
--local_max_consumers 10
--authkey superuser:amqpass
--amq_truststore_location /opt/oneops/inductor/lib/client.ts
--additional_java_args ""
--env_vars ""
```

After installing the inductor, the display service is started and the standalone OneOps upgrade is complete.

Updating an enterprise OneOps installation

Updating an enterprise OneOps installation takes a different approach for a few different reasons. First of all, in an enterprise installation all the services get installed on their own instances. Second, since an enterprise installation caters to an entire enterprise, stability, availability, and scalability are always an issue. So here are a few things that you should remember before you upgrade your enterprise installation:

- Ensure that you have your own Jenkins build server and it uploads the artifacts to your own `Nexus` repository. Ensure this `Nexus` repository is configured in the OneOps that manages your enterprise OneOps installation.
- Ensure that you use a stable build and not a release candidate or the master build.

This way, you will have a well-tested build for your enterprise.

- Make sure that your backup server is configured and OneOps is being regularly backed up.

- Although the downtime should be minimal to none, make sure that you do the upgrade during the least busy time to minimize the impact of any unforeseen events.

- If you have more than one OneOps installations, it is prudent to direct traffic to the second installation while one is being updated.

With these things in mind, the sequence for updating the various components is pretty much the same as updating a standalone OneOps installation. However, the steps involved are a bit different. The first thing you need to do, as mentioned earlier, is to choose an appropriate stable release that you want to deploy. Once you choose that, go to OneOps that manages your enterprise installation and click on the **OneOps assembly**. Select **Design** from the left-hand side menu and then select **Variables** from the center screen. From the numerous variables you see, the one that you want to modify is named **Version**. Click on it and then click on **Edit** in the upper right-hand corner:

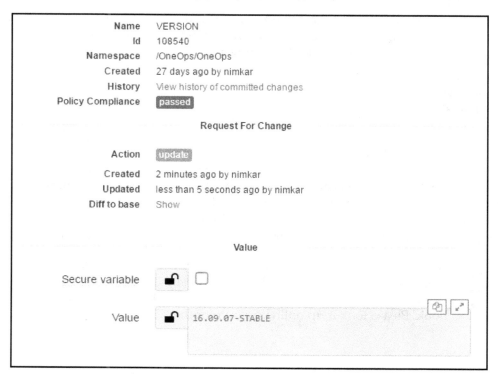

Click on **Save**. Once the changes are saved, you can go ahead and commit your changes. You will note that all the components derive their local version variable from the global version variable. At this point, if you click on **Transition** and attempt a deployment, OneOps will generate a deployment plan that will have the latest revision of all the components that need the upgrade. Go ahead and click on **Deploy**. OneOps should do the rest.

Configuring database backups

As seen so far, OneOps has a complex architecture and relies on many databases to provide optimum functionality as we have seen before. Again as with deployment, for database backup, the steps needed to back up a single machine installation and an enterprise installation are different.

Backing up a standalone OneOps installation

For a standalone installation, the three main `postgres` databases you need to back up are `activitidb`, `kloopzapp`, and `kloopzdb`. You can access these databases directly by logging in to your OneOps server and then doing a `sudo` as the `postgres` user:

```
# sudo su - postgres
-bash-4.2$ psql
Postgres=# l
```

Once you issue these commands, you can see these databases listed along with the default `postgres` database. Now you can design chef recipes to take backups or installation puppet or ansible and automate the backup process. However, in accordance with the *KISS* principle, the simplest way you can set up backups is to use the built-in `postgres` command. The `pg_dump` command for a single database backup or `pg_dumpall` for an all databases backup. You can add a **cron job** to run these commands nightly and another cron job to `scp` the dumped files to a secure server or a tape and delete the local copies.

 KISS is an acronym coined by the US Navy in 1960 for a design principle that states that systems work best if the design is kept simple and unnecessary complexity is avoided. I won't spell out the acronym in this book. Please look it up online. Search for the KISS principle.

As time goes by, your database size will also increase. To tackle that you can pipe your backup commands directly to a compression program:

```
pg_dumpall | gzip filename.gz
```

Similarly, you can restore the database by using the exact reverse of that command:

```
gunzip filename.gz | pg_restore
```

Backup an enterprise OneOps installation

Again an enterprise OneOps installation, as opposed to a standalone OneOps installation comes with backups built in. To make the backups work, you have to set up a few things correctly to begin with. First, you have to set up the BACKUP-HOST global variable to point to a host that has plenty of storage attached to it:

Name	BACKUP-HOST
Id	108542
Namespace	/OneOps/OneOps
Created	28 days ago by nimkar
History	View history of committed changes
Policy Compliance	passed

Value

Secure variable	🔓 ☐
Value	🔓 **changeme**

Once the variable is set, the value trickles down to the database components as local variables derived from the global variable. All backups taken are then copied to this host. For example, the following is the screenshot for this variable for CMSDB:

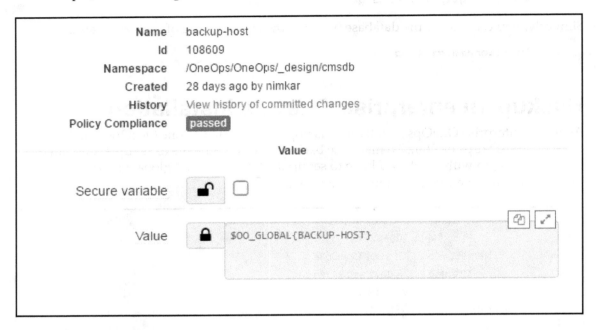

Once this is done, OneOps sets up automated jobs for database backups. These jobs are actually shell scripts, which are wrappers over chef recipes for the database snapshot backup.

Managing OneOps security

Once you have your OneOps setup for deployments, you can secure access to it in various ways. By default, OneOps allows users to create their own accounts and then log in with their accounts immediately after accepting the **End User License Agreement** (**EULA**). You can change this behavior by editing the setting in `settings.yml`. Specifically, if you set invitations to true, then users can register by invitation only. Also, if you set confirmation to true, then users will have to provide a valid e-mail address. A confirmation e-mail is sent to this address with a link on which they have to click to confirm their registration. Once they create their own ID, they can search for an organization and request to be added to it.

Managing OneOps groups

A group in OneOps is just a logical grouping of users. This is usually created by the group admin. Groups by themselves do not have any permissions associated to them. However, whole groups can be granted permissions by adding them to teams. A group can span across multiple organizations and hence a group name is always unique across the system. Technically, there is no limit on the number of users in a group. To create a group, simply click on your name and then click on the **Add Group** link. Provide an appropriate **Name** and **Description** for the group:

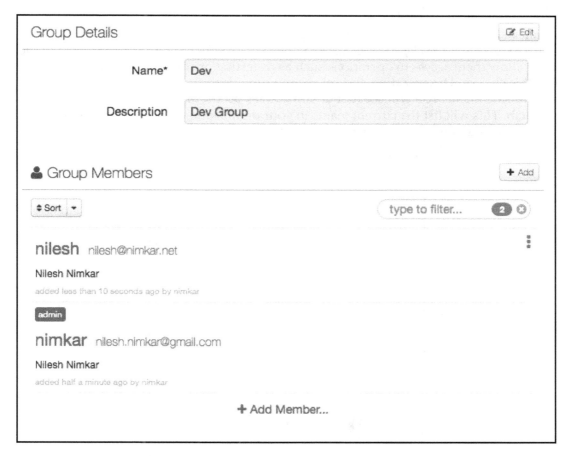

And then click on **Save**. Your group is ready to use. You can now add individual members to your group by clicking on **Add member**, as shown in the screenshot preceding.

Managing OneOps teams

As an admin, it is up to you to maintain various organizations and groups under it. As mentioned before, depending on the size of your company and your installation an organization can be an umbrella that can either encompass the whole company, a particular department, a development team, or even smaller segregated entities. This logical segregation is entirely up to you and should be planned very carefully. Once an organization is created, you can create teams under it and assign various roles to the group. An admin team is provided by default, and whoever created the organization is added to the admin team by default.

You can also create teams with specific purposes and access. For example, you may want to create a team called *Developers* with access to design assemblies and request transition them but not allow them access to operations such as restarting or stopping and starting services. To do this click on **Organization** and select your organization, then click on **Settings** in the left-hand side menu. You will see that organization's profile and settings. Click on the **Teams** tab. This will list the current teams in your organization. You should see the default **admins** team and any other teams that you may have created:

Click on the **Add** button or the **Add Team** link. Select an appropriate **Name** for the team such as *developers*. Now select the appropriate access for the team. The **Access Control** is split into three categories. **Access Management**, **Cloud Permissions**, and **Assembly Permissions**. Under **Access Management**, you have **Manage Access**. If selected, members in this team will be able to grant access to others when they themselves are granted access to an assembly or a cloud. In addition, it also allows members to create new clouds and assemblies. You can go ahead and select this as you may want to give developers access to create their own assemblies and then grant others access to these assemblies. In addition, you also want developers to create their own clouds as developers may want to test locally by creating Vagrant and Docker clouds. The second option that you can select is **Organization Scope**. If selected, this grants everyone in this team access to all assemblies and clouds within this organization. You may or may not want to select this depending on the granularity of the access you want to maintain. In theory for developers, you should not select this as the theory of least privileges states that for security, developers should have only enough access to allow them to perform their tasks.

Next in **Cloud permissions**, you can select **services**, **compliance**, or **support**. Selecting **services** allows the members of this team to add, modify, or delete services from clouds that they have access to. In turn, if you have selected **Organization Scope**, then they will be able to do this in every cloud under this team. It is important that you select this option if you want your developers to be able to add services to clouds that they create. Next is **compliance**. Compliance and support are very similar in functionality. If you select **compliance**, you can then go to a particular cloud in this organization and add the compliance object to the cloud. To do this, click on **clouds** on the left-hand side menu. In the center menu, you should see a tab named **compliance**. Click on it and then click on **Add**. Select an appropriate **Name** for the compliance policy. Compliance policies are applied to every deployment at the time of deployment if the compliance object is added to the cloud to which the deployment is happening and the team that is doing the deployment has the compliance rights:

Provide an appropriate **Name** for the compliance object. You can enable and disable the compliance object by selecting the **Enable** checkbox. If the **Deployment Approval** checkbox is selected, besides executing the compliance object, during deployment, OneOps also asks a member of team for the approval, depending on how the backend communication is configured. Anyone belonging to a team with compliance checked can look at the results of compliance and approve the deployment. Finally, you can provide a script to be executed and the filter. The script is downloaded and executed against each and every CI in the deployment. If you do not wish to execute the script against every CI, you can provide a filter and filter out the CIs that you do not wish the script to execute against.

Next is **support**. That is reserved for support and DevOps group. Developers do not need access to support object or services, so you can leave that unchecked for now. In assembly permissions, you have design, transition, and operations. The developer group will need design permission, this will allow them to add, update, and delete platforms and variables from assemblies. The developer group will also need the transition permission. This gives them permission to perform a wide array of tasks. The team will be able to add, update, and delete an environment. They will be able to add, update, and delete component monitor thresholds. They will be able to update components and variables in an environment. They will also be able to pull and force pull releases, commit releases, and do deployments. If a different team has been given DevOps access, the team will still have to approve deployments before a deployment can proceed.

Similarly, let's say you want to create a DevOps team that takes care of all your systems, that is operations ready, that has access across the production environment, that has rights across the production environment to perform actions such as stop, start, and adjust thresholds, and that has the final say in deployments by providing relevant approvals for some environments such as production, here is how you can do it. Again follow the same steps that you followed to create the developer group. Click on your **Organization** and then click on **Settings**, **Teams**, then **Add**. Give your team a meaningful name such as **DevOps**. Now set up permissions for the group:

For the **DevOps** group, you will have to set up permissions a little differently as compared with the developer group.

```
Manage Access        ☐
                     🔍 When checked and this team is assigned to a cloud or an assembly it
                     allows team members to manage other team assignments. Additionally,
                     when checked it allows team members to create new clouds and
                     assemblies.

Organization Scope   ☑
                     🏛 When checked this team will automatically have access to all assemblies
                     and clouds in the organization (without the need to assign it explicitly and
                     governed by the permissions specified below

                              Cloud Permissions

Allow Modification In    ☐    ⚙    services
                         ☐    💼    compliance
                         ☑    📇    support

                            Assembly Permissions

Allow Modification In    ☐    🕸    design
                         ☑    ⊙    transition
                         ☑    ...ı  operations
```

Depending on your organization's policies and structure, you may or may not want to give **Manage Access** permission to the **DevOpsgroup**. If you do, then the **DevOps** group will also be responsible for adding and managing clouds and other CI in the OneOps system. You should definitely select the **Organization Scope** checkbox as this will give access to the team to all the clouds and assemblies under the organization without having to explicitly add them to each one of them. Next under **Cloud Permissions**, you should select **support**. If you select **support**, then you will also need to add the support object to the relevant clouds. To do this, click on the **Clouds** link in the left-hand side menu and then select the **Cloud** to which you want to add the object. You should see a support tab. Click on it and then click on the **Add Support** link or the button. Give the support object a meaningful name again such as **DevOps**.

In **Description**, give a good description as this will be displayed during each deployment to the user. You can enable or disable the approvals by selecting the state here. And finally, select **Deployment Approval** if you want each deployment to require approval:

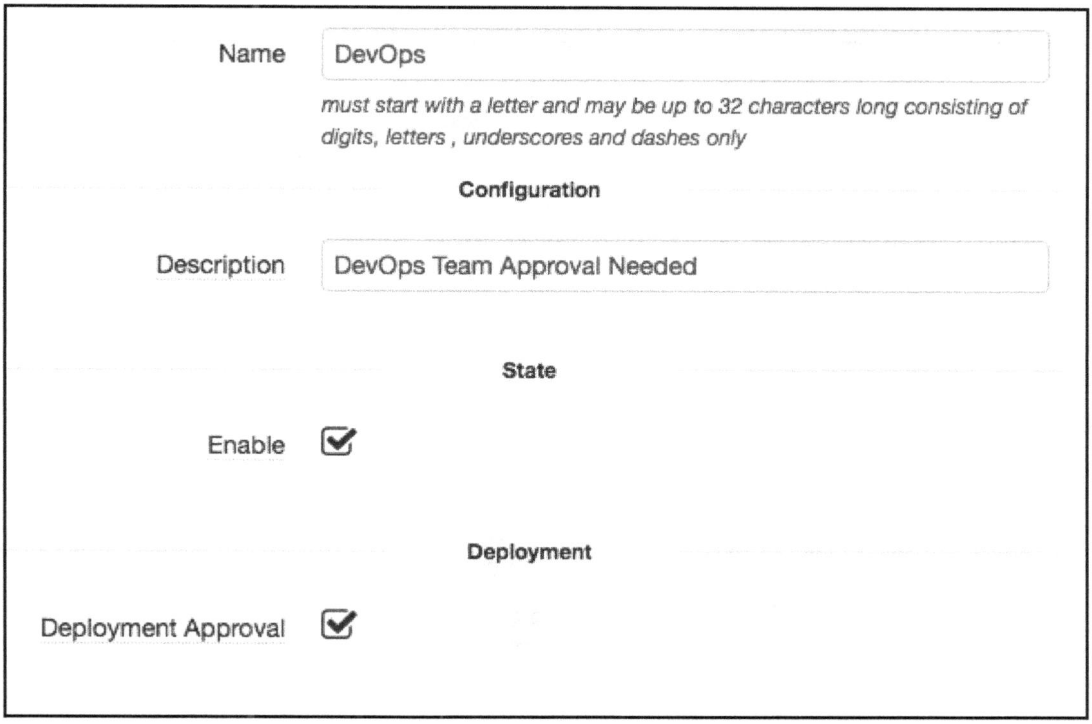

Name	DevOps

must start with a letter and may be up to 32 characters long consisting of digits, letters , underscores and dashes only

Configuration

Description	DevOps Team Approval Needed

State

Enable	☑

Deployment

Deployment Approval	☑

Once this is added to the Cloud, each deployment that happens to that cloud will need to be approved by the DevOps team. Finally, in **Assembly Permission**, the DevOps team does not need the design permission as the DevOps team will not be making any changes to the assembly design. However, as an operations team, DevOps will need access to transition and operations, so be sure to select those. Once all of this are done, click on **Save**. You now have two teams created, **Developers** and **DevOps**. Once your teams are ready, you can either add users individually or you can add groups to save you from adding users individually:

There is a difference between a group and a team. A group, by default, does not have any permissions attached to it and only get certain rights after being added to a team. Also, note that you cannot add one team to another team.

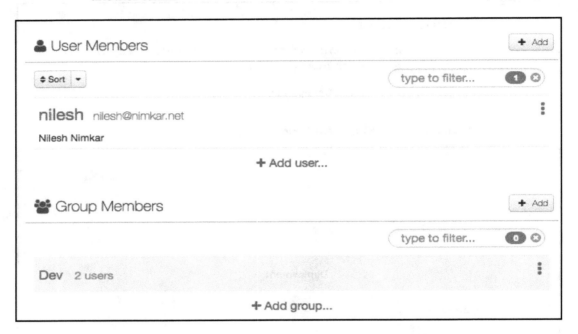

Summary

In this chapter, we saw how to manage your OneOps installation, be it standalone or enterprise. Although the overheads of installation for an enterprise installation are a bit more, most of the management tasks are automated. On the other hand, for most small shops a standalone OneOps installation is more than enough to handle all their needs; however, most of the management tasks have to be manually set up. We saw tasks such as upgrading and what exactly happens in the background, database backups, and creating users, groups, and teams. In the next chapter, we will go a little deeper into OneOps backend structure and take a look at inductors and circuits and see exactly what makes OneOps tick.

7
Working with Functional Components

In the previous chapter, we saw how to manage your OneOps installations, whether standalone or enterprise. We also looked at various tasks such as upgrade and backup and what exactly happens when they are triggered. Let's look at a few of the important components of the background and how they fit into the overall operation of OneOps, namely the inductor and the circuit, which do most of the work in OneOps.

Inductor and its structure

Inductor, as explained earlier, forms the link between the design and deployments. The inductor is responsible for collecting the two types of order, `WorkOrder` and `ActionOrder`, from the controller from various queues by zone. It then executes various actions based on the type of order. Remember that `WorkOrder` always results in a physical change of a CI-like deployment or in a teardown of CI, whereas `ActionOrder` will result in the change of the state of a CI-like stop, start, or restart. The inductor consumes these orders and acts on them by executing them either locally or remotely. The local execution is done via an Chef-solo cookbooks, and the remote execution is handled via SSH Chef-solo execution.

By default, the inductor component gets installed in `/opt/oneops/inductor`.

```
[ooadmin@ip-172-31-52-21 inductor]$ ls -l
total 4
lrwxrwxrwx. 1 ooadmin ooadmin 35 Nov 15 19:02 circuit-oneops-1 -> /home/oneops/b
uild/circuit-oneops-1
drwxr-xr-x. 4 ooadmin ooadmin 37 Nov 16 03:41 clouds-available
drwxr-xr-x. 2 ooadmin ooadmin 37 Nov 16 03:41 clouds-enabled
drwxr-xr-x. 2 ooadmin ooadmin 21 Sep  7 22:40 init.d
drwxr-xr-x. 2 ooadmin ooadmin 22 Sep  7 22:40 lib
drwxr-xr-x. 2 ooadmin ooadmin  6 Sep  7 22:40 log
drwxr-xr-x. 3 ooadmin ooadmin 80 Sep  7 22:40 shared
-rw-r--r--. 1 ooadmin ooadmin  7 Sep  7 22:40 user
[ooadmin@ip-172-31-52-21 inductor]$
```

Although you can set up your own inductor, it is highly recommended that you retain the default inductor setup that comes with OneOps. A single inductor can manage multiple clouds and multiple zones. However, should you decide to set up your own inductor in a different directory, it's important that you understand the layout of the inductor as seen in the earlier directory. The most important directory in inductor is the `circuit-oneops-1` directory. This is linked to the circuit directory under the build directory in OneOps home. This is a good design as now you only have to update your circuit in one place and all your inductors will get updated. If you do not use this design, you would have to update each of your inductors manually. The `clouds-available` directory shows you all the clouds that are available to you. The `clouds-enabled` directory has all the clouds that are currently enabled. When a cloud is enabled, inductor creates a link from the `clouds-available` directory to the `cloud-enabled` directory. By default, a shared cloud is created that is available to everyone. `init.d` has an `init` script, which is added to the server's `init` scripts, so the inductor is started and stopped whenever the server starts, stops, and restarts. Under the `lib` directory, you will find the trust store that houses the keys used by inductor to connect to the various queues used by the clouds. Finally, `shared` has the actual libraries and cookbooks that execute various tasks for inductor. If you look under `clouds-enabled` or `shared`, you will find a very similar directory structure.

```
[ooadmin@ip-172-31-52-21 inductor]$ ls -l
total 4
lrwxrwxrwx. 1 ooadmin ooadmin 35 Nov 15 19:02 circuit-oneops-1 -> /home/oneops/b
uild/circuit-oneops-1
drwxr-xr-x. 4 ooadmin ooadmin 37 Nov 16 03:41 clouds-available
drwxr-xr-x. 2 ooadmin ooadmin 37 Nov 16 03:41 clouds-enabled
drwxr-xr-x. 2 ooadmin ooadmin 21 Sep  7 22:40 init.d
drwxr-xr-x. 2 ooadmin ooadmin 22 Sep  7 22:40 lib
drwxr-xr-x. 2 ooadmin ooadmin  6 Sep  7 22:40 log
drwxr-xr-x. 3 ooadmin ooadmin 80 Sep  7 22:40 shared
-rw-r--r--. 1 ooadmin ooadmin  7 Sep  7 22:40 user
[ooadmin@ip-172-31-52-21 inductor]$
```

A few directories to note here are `conf`, `log`, and `logstash-forwarder`. When connecting to a particular cloud's queue, inductor will look into the cloud's `conf` directory and try to find a file named `inductor.properties`. The configuration specified in the file will then be used to connect to the queues for that cloud. If you create a custom cloud and want to create a separate inductor to connect to it, you must specify a configuration like the one found here. A good starting point is to look at the configuration for the shared cloud and then customize it for your own cloud.

```
[root@ip-172-31-52-21 conf]# more inductor.properties
amq.connect_string = failover:(ssl://localhost:61617?keepAlive=true)?jms.useCompres
sion=true&initialReconnectDelay=1000&maxReconnectAttempts=-1&startupMaxReconnectAtt
empts=0&jms.prefetchPolicy.queuePrefetch=1
amq.zone = superuser
amq.authkey = amqpass
amq.in_queue = shared.ind-wo
packer_home = /opt/oneops/inductor/packer
data_dir = /opt/oneops/inductor/clouds-available/shared/data
scan_path = /opt/oneops/inductor/clouds-available/shared/retry
scan_period = 5
retry_count = 2
ip_attribute = public_ip
mgmt_domain = localhost
perf_collector_cert_location = /etc/pki/tls/logstash/certs/logstash-forwarder.crt
mgmt_url = http://localhost:9090
mgmt_cert = /etc/pki/tls/logstash/certs/logstash-forwarder.crt
daq_enabled = true
dns = on
debug_mode = on
max_consumers = 10
local_max_consumers = 10
env_vars =
tunnel_metrics = on
[root@ip-172-31-52-21 conf]#
```

The `logs` directory contains the log for this cloud. Each cloud maintains its own log. This log is then picked up by the `logstash-forwarder` and forwarded to port `5000` and then on to the logserver for processing. On a single-server installation, it's the same machine, and on an enterprise, it installs a dedicated instance. OneOps also installs `oneops admins gem`, which makes the `inductor` command available. This makes managing inductors easy.

 To manage an inductor, you must look into that inductor's directory first. Also, inductor is created as the `ooadmin` user, and you must use `sudo` as that user to run any inductor commands.

Running just the `inductor` command shows all the options available under an inductor. The most common command you will use will be `inductor tail`, which will show you the log for an inductor and continuously tail it.

```
[ooadmin@ip-172-31-52-21 inductor]$ inductor
Commands:
  inductor add                               # Add cloud to the inductor
  inductor check                             # Inductor check
  inductor check_agent                       # Inductor check logstash forwarder
  inductor create                            # Creates and configures a new in...
  inductor disable PATTERN                   # Disable inductor clouds matchin...
  inductor enable PATTERN                    # Enable inductor clouds matching...
  inductor force_stop NAME                   # Inductor force stop (will kill -9)
  inductor help [COMMAND]                    # Describe available commands or ...
  inductor install_initd                     # Install /etc/init.d/inductor
  inductor list [PATTERN]                    # List clouds in the inductor
  inductor restart NAME                      # Inductor restart
  inductor restart_logstash_forwarder NAME   # Inductor logstash agent restart
  inductor start NAME                        # Inductor start
  inductor start_logstash_forwarder NAME     # Inductor logstash agent start
  inductor status                            # Inductor status
  inductor status_logstash_forwarder NAME    # Inductor logstash agent status
  inductor stop NAME                         # Inductor stop (will finish proc...
  inductor stop_logstash_forwarder NAME      # Inductor logstash agent stop
  inductor tail                              # Inductor log tail

[ooadmin@ip-172-31-52-21 inductor]$ ▌
```

Build, install, and configure an inductor

Most of the time, you will be building and installing an inductor as part of the overall OneOps build or upgrade, be it standalone or enterprise. However, sometimes, you might want to upgrade just the inductor. You can use the steps given later to do so. For that, you will need to clone two git repositories--the `oneops-admin` and the `inductor` repositories. Choose a place of your liking on the server where you want to upgrade the inductor and clone the two repositories:

```
git clone https://github.com/oneops/inductor.git
git clone https://github.com/oneops/oneops-admin.git
```

Now go into the `inductor` directory and build it with the `mvn` command:

```
mvn clean package
```

After building it, it should create a directory named `target` with a file named `inductor-<version>.jar`. Open the `oneops-admin` directory, create a directory named `target`, and copy this jar into that directory. Now build the `oneops-admin` gem. This gem encapsulates the inductor gem. If the gem builds successfully, you can go ahead and install it:

```
gem build oneops-admin.gemspec
gem install oneops-admin-VERSION.gem
```

Now that we have some background on inductor, let's create a secure cloud and hook up a separate inductor, which is different from the shared inductor to which it is connected. This way all the `WorkOrders` and `ActionOrders` for our secure cloud are routed through our inductor instead of the shared inductor, and we can keep track of the secure log. To begin with, let's create an empty cloud and call it **SecureCloud**. The name is not important; we are calling it **SecureCloud** to emphasize the fact that we would like to route the traffic from this cloud separately instead of from the shared inductor. Log in to your OneOps instance and click on **Clouds** on the left-hand side menu, then click on the **Add Cloud** button or link. The **Add Cloud** screen will appear. Choose the name **SecureCloud** or any other name you prefer. Remember this name because OneOps creates a queue by this name, and you will be asked the queue name when you create the inductor. For the location, let's select **Vagrant** because this is the easiest cloud to create. However, these instructions will apply to any cloud you choose.

Now click on **Save**. That's all you should need to create an empty cloud. Now you can go ahead and create a separate inductor at the backend and hook it up to the cloud. SSH into your OneOps instance and then log in as the ooadmin user. Remember that an inductor gets installed as an ooadmin user, and all inductor commands must be run as ooadmin. Go to the directory /opt/oneops/inductor and run the command inductor add. You will be asked to enter various options.

 If you are having difficulty choosing the various options, you will find a file named inductor_answers in the directory /home/oneops. You can always use it as a reference.

```
[ooadmin@ip-172-31-52-21 inductor]$ inductor add
[Manage dns? (on or off - defaults to off) on
[Debug mode? (keeps ssh keys and doesn't terminate compute on compute::add failure.
on or off - defaults to off) on
[Metrics collections? (if empty defaults to false)? true
[What collector domain (the domain of your forge or collector)? localhost
[Tunnel metrics thru ssh tunnel (defaults to off)? on
[Perf Collector cert file location ? (If empty defaults to local cloud cert) /etc/pk
i/tls/logstash/certs/logstash-forwarder.crt
[What compute attribute to use for the ip to connect (if empty defaults to private_i
p)? public_ip
[Queue? SecureCloud
[URL to the UI? http://localhost:9090
[Logstash cert file location ? (If empty defaults to local cloud cert) /etc/pki/tls/
logstash/certs/logstash-forwarder.crt
[Comma seperated list of logstash host:port ? (if empty defaults to localhost:5000)
vagrant.oo.com:5000
[Max Consumers? 10
[Max Local Consumers (ones for iaas)? 10
[What is the authorization key? superuser:amqpass
[Additional Java args (default empty)?
[Environment Variables to pass to Executor (default empty)?
Location of TrustStore to connect AMQ (If empty no trustStore is used)? /opt/oneops
/inductor/lib/client.ts
```

The following are all the options that inductor asks you, with a brief explanation of each:

1. The first thing inductor asks you is if it should manage DNS for you. It defaults to off; in our case, we chose on.

2. It asks if it should turn debug mode on (default is off). If the debug mode is turned on, then if, for any reason, a compute node fails to add, it does not get rolled back and the corresponding SSH keys do not get deleted. They are left alone for you to debug.

3. The inductor asks you if it should collect metrics. We are choosing `true`. Default is `false`.

4. It asks for your domain of forge or collector. In our case, it's localhost. If you are doing an enterprise install, you must provide the instance name of your collector.

5. It asks if it should tunnel metrics through ssl. Default is `off`. We are turning it `on`. This is a safe thing to do in case we are deploying on a public cloud; we don't want anyone snooping on our metrics.

6. It asks for the `Perf Collector certificate` file. Unless you move it around, it should be in the standard path of `/etc/pki/tls/logstash/certs/logstash-forwarder.crt`, where OneOps installs it.

7. It asks if it should connect to compute instances on a public IP or a private IP. We are choosing a public IP.

8. It asks for the `queue` name. Since we are hooking this inductor to the cloud that we just created, the queue name will be the same as the cloud name, which is `SecureCloud`.

9. It asks for the URL for the UI, which is `http://localhost:9090` or `localhost:3000`, or a different URL, if you did an enterprise installation.

10. It asks for the `Logstash certificate` file location, which is the same as the `Perf Collector certificate` file.

11. It asks for your `logstash` host and port. We entered `vagrant.oo.com:5000`. If you check the `hosts` file, this host is aliased to localhost.

12. It will ask for the maximum consumers for inductor as well as maximum local consumers. We choose `10` for both.

13. For the authorization key, we choose the default key `superuser:amqpass`. If you wish to secure your clouds and change your `amq` installation so that your `amq` username and password are different than default, then you must change the password in `/opt/activemq/conf/credentials.conf` and restart the `activemq` server.

14. It will then ask you for additional JVM and environment variable arguments. In our case, we choose to keep them empty.

15. Finally, you will be asked to enter the trust store that will be used to connect to the `activemq` broker. You can find this at `/opt/oneops/inductor/lib/client.ts`.

After entering all these details, you should see a bunch of `create` messages, and ultimately, you should see success. It will also show you the next steps to run, namely the commands `inductor start` and then `inductor tail`. If all goes well, you should see log messages showing that your inductor successfully started and connected to your cloud's queue.

```
2016-11-16 06:00:53,746  INFO    Config:301       using dns config: /opt/oneops/induc
tor/global/dns.conf
2016-11-16 06:00:53,746  INFO    Config:318       not a public inductor - missing: /o
pt/oneops/inductor/global/dns.conf
2016-11-16 06:00:53,962  INFO    CachingConnectionFactory:311    Established shared
JMS Connection: ActiveMQConnection {id=ID:ip-172-31-52-21.ec2.internal-51803-147927
6053858-1:1,clientId=null,started=false}
2016-11-16 06:00:54,243  INFO    FailoverTransport:1065  Successfully connected to s
sl://localhost:61617?keepAlive=true
2016-11-16 06:00:54,332  INFO    Listener:146    /opt/oneops/inductor/clouds-availab
le/SecureCloud/data free space mb: 20566
2016-11-16 06:00:54,332  INFO    Listener:92     Inductor{ Config{ ipAddr='172.31.52
.21 (eth0)', circuitDir='/opt/oneops/inductor/packer', inQueue='SecureCloud.ind-wo'
, retryCount=2, ipAttribute='public_ip', dataDir='/opt/oneops/inductor/clouds-avail
able/SecureCloud/data', mgmtDomain='localhost', perfCollectorCertLocation='/etc/pki
/tls/logstash/certs/logstash-forwarder.crt', mgmtUrl='http://localhost:9090', mgmtC
ert='/etc/pki/tls/logstash/certs/logstash-forwarder.crt', dnsEnabled='on', dnsDisab
led=false, dnsConfigFile='/opt/oneops/inductor/global/dns.conf', debugMode='on', lo
calMaxConsumers=10, rsyncTimeout=30, bomClasses=[bom.fqdn, bom.lb], rfcActions=[del
ete], cmdTimeout=10, stubbedCloudsList=[], stubResponseTimeInSeconds=5, stubResultC
ode=1, env=}, semaphore=java.util.concurrent.Semaphore@343570b7[Permits = 10]}
2016-11-16 06:00:54,340  INFO    DefaultLifecycleProcessor:341   Starting beans in p
hase 2147483647
2016-11-16 06:00:54,400  INFO    FailoverTransport:1065  Successfully connected to s
sl://localhost:61617?keepAlive=true
```

Here is what all our steps have achieved in the background. If you go to the `/opt/oneops/inductor/clouds-available` directory, you will see two directories, namely `shared` and `SecureCloud`. You will also see the same directories under `/opt/oneops/inductor/clouds-enabled`,since these are just links to the directories under `clouds-enabled` and our cloud named `SecureCloud` was successfully added and enabled on this inductor. If you go into the `SecureCloud` directory under `clouds-enabled` (or `clouds-available`, which are one and the same), you will see the directory structure is quite similar to a shared structure. Under `log`, you will find a file named `inductor.log`, which will have log messages exclusive to `SecureCloud`. Any services you add to the cloud will have their `WorkOrders` and `ActionOrder` routed via this inductor. Any logs produced will also be exclusively logged to this inductor. If you go to the `conf` directory, you will see all the configuration we were prompted for were added to the `inductor.properties` file, except for the `Activemq` broker trust store, which was added to the `vmargs` file.

Now you can also run commands on the inductor independently of each other, including stopping, starting, and looking up statuses as well as disabling them.

```
[ooadmin@ip-172-31-52-21 inductor]$ inductor status
586
  consumer ok   shared
734
  consumer ok   SecureCloud
[ooadmin@ip-172-31-52-21 inductor]$ inductor stop SecureCloud
        stop  SecureCloud consumer
        stop  logstash agent /opt/oneops/inductor/clouds-enabled/SecureCloud
[ooadmin@ip-172-31-52-21 inductor]$ inductor status
586
  consumer ok   shared
consumer down  SecureCloud
[ooadmin@ip-172-31-52-21 inductor]$ inductor disable SecureCloud
      disable  SecureCloud
[ooadmin@ip-172-31-52-21 inductor]$ inductor status
586
  consumer ok   shared
[ooadmin@ip-172-31-52-21 inductor]$ █
```

Running `inductor stop SecureCloud` will stop the `SecureCloud` inductor, and no `WorkOrders` or `ActionOrders` will be routed to this inductor. You can also remove inductor by running `inductor disable SecureCloud`. This leaves a copy of the inductor in the `clouds-available`, directory but removes it from the `clouds-enabled` directory. To completely remove all traces of the inductor, simply delete the directory `SecureCloud` from the `clouds-available` directory. You are then free to delete the cloud from OneOps too, provided no services are added to it.

What are circuits?

We briefly touched on the `circuit` directory in the previous section. The default circuit that comes installed with OneOps is named `circuit-oneops-1` and can be found in the inductor directory `/opt/oneops/inductor`.

In the early days of OneOps, circuits used to be called **packs** before they were renamed as circuits. Now the name circuit or pack is used interchangeably.

A `circuit` directory has three main subdirectories--`components`, `clouds`, and `packs` (or circuits in the latest terminology)

```
[[root@ip-172-31-52-21 circuit-oneops-1]# ls -l
total 24
drwxr-xr-x. 2 root root 4096 Sep 29 21:15 catalogs
-rw-r--r--. 1 root root  314 Sep  7 22:32 CHANGELOG.md
drwxr-xr-x. 2 root root 4096 Nov 16 20:13 clouds
drwxr-xr-x. 4 root root   36 Sep  7 22:32 components
-rw-r--r--. 1 root root   60 Sep  7 22:32 Gemfile
drwxr-xr-x. 3 root root 4096 Nov 16 20:46 packs
-rw-r--r--. 1 root root  171 Sep  7 22:32 README.md
[root@ip-172-31-52-21 circuit-oneops-1]#
```

The `clouds` directory contains definitions for various clouds and the services provided by them. The `packs` directory contains the actual circuit definition for various platforms that can be added to the assemblies and the dependencies between them. In general, everything under the circuit is defined and managed using Chef-specific Ruby **Domain-Specific Language** (**DSL**).

A DSL is a language built for a specific purpose using an underlying language. You usually don't need to learn the details of the underlying language to learn DSL, and can come up to speed very quickly. For example, Rails is DSL, specifically built for web development using Ruby, and you need very basic knowledge of Ruby to learn Rails. Similarly, Chef is a DSL for DevOps tasks built using Ruby.

The `clouds` directory provides a template for all the clouds that OneOps plugs into. Each cloud also lists all the service it provides, along with the *type* of service that it is. For every cloud that is supported and every service that is added, a corresponding cookbook needs to be added in the `components` directory. Currently, the definition is in Chef, as are the cookbooks with support for Puppet and Ansible coming very soon.

```
name "aws"
description "Amazon Web Services"
auth "awssecretkey"

service "ebs",
  :cookbook => 'ebs',
  :source => [Chef::Config[:register], Chef::Config[:version].split(".").first].joi
n('.'),
  :provides => { :service => 'storage' }

service "elb",
  :cookbook => 'elb',
  :source => [Chef::Config[:register], Chef::Config[:version].split(".").first].joi
n('.'),
  :provides => { :service => 'lb' }

service "s3",
  :cookbook => 's3',
  :source => [Chef::Config[:register], Chef::Config[:version].split(".").first].joi
n('.'),
  :provides => { :service => 'filestore' }

service "route53",
  :cookbook => 'route53',
@
"aws.rb" 28L, 932C
```

The `packs` directory comes with a wide variety of software already built in. This is the software that you see in the list when you add a platform to your assembly. The `doc` directory under `packs` contains images that get displayed when an assembly is added in the GUI. We will cover this in detail when we create a custom pack in the later chapters. For now, you only need to understand that circuits are defined as models of what resources and components are required and what are optional for it to be installed and to be functional.

These models are defined by two relationships--`depends_on` and `managed_by`. For example, a PHP circuit requires Apache circuit to function properly, that is, it `depends_on` Apache, which in turn `depends_on` the operating system, which in turn `depends_on` a compute instance. We will also look at these relationships in detail when we define a custom circuit.

```
# depends_on
[ { :from => 'php',      :to => 'os' },
  { :from => 'php',      :to => 'apache' },
  { :from => 'php',      :to => 'library' },
  { :from => 'php',      :to => 'download'},
  { :from => 'phpapp',   :to => 'php'     },
  { :from => 'website',  :to => 'phpapp'  },
  { :from => 'website',  :to => 'php'     } ].each do |link|
  relation "#{link[:from]}::depends_on::#{link[:to]}",
    :relation_name => 'DependsOn',
    :from_resource => link[:from],
    :to_resource   => link[:to],
    :attributes    => { "flex" => false, "min" => 1, "max" => 1 }
end


# managed_via
[ 'php', 'phpapp' ].each do |from|
  relation "#{from}::managed_via::compute",
    :except => [ '_default' ],
    :relation_name => 'ManagedVia',
    :from_resource => from,
    :to_resource   => 'compute',
    :attributes    => { }
end
```

 If you see the default circuit directory, `circuit-oneops-1`, you will also see another directory named `catalogs`, which has prefabricated blueprints of commonly used installations, such as **CloudFoundry**, **Wordpress**, and **Oracle**. However, as of writing this, these have not kept pace with the updates made to OneOps, and are unusable with the latest version of OneOps. This, however, may change in the future, so keep an eye on them.

The `components` directory has cookbooks and modules. Currently, only cookbooks are in use because, for backend, OneOps supports only Chef; however, Puppet support is coming very soon. The `modules` directory has a test Puppet module that is a test work order that is unused. The `cookbooks` directory contains cookbooks for all the circuits as well as the clouds. Many directories also have a README.md file giving a short explanation about the cookbook and its functionality.

Working with circuits

When we installed the OneOps admin gem, it installed two commands for us--inductor and `circuit`. As the `inductor` command is used to control the inductor, the `circuit` command, predictably, is used to control the circuit. However, like the inductor, the circuit is not an application that runs in the background. As a matter of fact, any change that you make to the circuit or if you create a new circuit, they must be synced with the CMSDB, and that is the prime application of the `circuit` command. The `circuit` command should also be run from within a circuit and with sufficient privileges. Running just `circuit` will show you the usage of the `circuit` command. Running `circuit help <command>` will show the help for the command.

```
[root@ip-172-31-52-21 circuit-oneops-1]# circuit
Commands:
  circuit clouds          # Clouds Sync
  circuit create          # Setup Environment for cookbook/Pack creation
  circuit help [COMMAND]  # Describe available commands or one specific command
  circuit init            # Initialize the circuit
  circuit install         # Install the circuit
  circuit model           # Model Sync
  circuit packs           # Pack Sync
  circuit register        # Register source

[root@ip-172-31-52-21 circuit-oneops-1]#
```

The `circuit cloud` command will sync all the changes made to all the clouds, `circuit model` syncs all the changes made to the models or the cookbooks, and `circuit packs` syncs all the changes made to the packs. `circuit install` will sync all the changes made to the circuit. Under the hood, the `circuit` command calls a command called `knife` to do the heavy lifting.

If you are familiar with Chef, you will recognize the `knife` command as the command used to manage the cookbooks and data bags from a workstation to the Chef server. You can see the configuration for the Chef server in the `chef/knife.rb`. In our case, it is running on localhost on port 4000. Feel free to change the address to an appropriate instance if you are on an enterprise or a different install.

However, before we look at the sample `knife` commands, let's try and sync up the `while` circuit. Change into the `circuit` directory and run the command shown here:

```
cd /opt/oneops/inductor/ circuit-oneops-1
circuit install
```

```
package_name: catalog
package_name: bom
package_name: manifest
Processing metadata for zookeeper from /home/oneops/build/circuit-oneops-1/componen
ts/cookbooks/zookeeper/metadata.rb
Skipping metadata for class zookeeper since --relations option is specified
package_name: mgmt.catalog
package_name: mgmt.manifest
package_name: catalog
package_name: manifest
package_name: bom
Metadata cache status update http response code : 200
Model synced!
        running  knife register
Ensuring namespace /public exists
Registering source oneops in namespace /public
Updating source oneops
Successfuly registered source oneops
Successfuly created packs namespace for source oneops
Source registered!
        running  knife pack sync -a
source: /public/oneops/packs
Pack apache version 1 matches signature 120304fe5847fb61a0b564fd5f035d54, use --rel
oad to force load.
source: /public/oneops/packs
Pack cassandra version 1 matches signature 7dc4fc6fa57b32e79a1b564f6e11da78, use --
```

As you can see, it will sync all the individual parts of the circuit one by one with the CMSDB and the Chef server. It will also show you the individual `knife` commands that it is calling in the background for you.

Now let's make a change to a circuit. If we install a PHP pack, we will see that the choices available to us in terms of installation version are **5.5.30**, **5.5.37**, **5.5.38**, and **default**, which happens to be **5.3.3**:

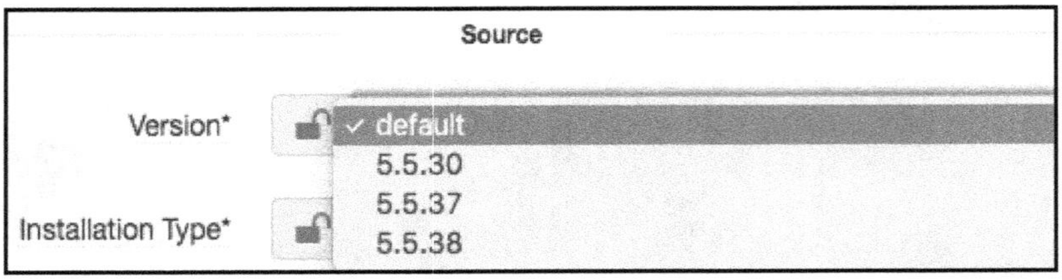

However, at the time of writing this, the latest PHP version was 5.6.28. Let's say that we want to add 5.6.28 as a binary installable option in OneOps. We can easily do so by editing and uploading the PHP model:

1. Edit the file `circuit-oneops-1/components/cookbooks/php/metadata.rb` and add the version number to the form field, as shown here:

```
description        "Installs/Configures PHP"
version            "0.1"
maintainer         "OneOps"
maintainer_email   "support@oneops.com"
license            "Apache License, Version 2.0"

grouping 'default',
  :access => "global",
  :packages => [ 'base', 'mgmt.catalog', 'catalog', 'mgmt.manifest', 'manifest', 'bom
' ]

# installation attributes

attribute 'version',
  :description => 'Version',
  :required => 'required',
  :default => '5.3.3',
  :format => {
    :important => true,
    :help => 'PHP Version',
    :category => '1.Source',
    :order => 1,
    :form => {'field' => 'select', 'options_for_select' => [['default', 'default'], [
'5.5.30', '5.5.30'], ['5.5.37', '5.5.37'], ['5.5.38', '5.5.38'], ['5.6.28', '5.6.28']
]}
```

2. Save the file and then run the following commands from the root directory of your circuit that is, `circuit-oneops-1`. If you are running an enterprise install, or if your CMSAPI server is different than `cmsapi`, then replace `cmsapi` with the appropriate instance name:

```
export CMSAPI=http://cmsapi:8080
knife model sync php
curl http://cmsapi:8080/transistor/rest/cache/md/clear
/etc/init.d/display restart
```

3. The `cmsapi` variable ensures that you are pointing to the correct `cmsapi` sever. The `knife model sync` command will sync all changes made to the PHP model to the CMS server and the Chef server. The `curl` command clears the transistor cache of any cached metadata. This is very important as we have made a single change to the metadata file. Finally, restarting the display will clear any Rails cache. You must run the last command as root. If not, you should run it with `sudo`.

4. Load a previous assembly that contains the PHP platform, or else create a brand-new assembly and add the PHP platform. If you click on the design diagram of a previous assembly, you may have to do a force pull of the pack design before you proceed to the next step. Click on the PHP component of the app and then click on **edit**. You will now find that your PHP version is a selectable option in the drop-down menu for PHP.

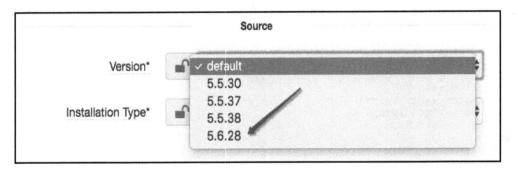

Summary

In this chapter, you learned about *inductors* and *circuits*. You also had a brief introduction to how each functions, and made changes to both inductors and circuits. Inductors and circuits form the functional core of OneOps. We saw how an inductor processes the different kinds of orders. We also briefly saw how a circuit stores all the components and clouds under it. In the upcoming chapters, we will also see how to add a custom cloud and add it to OneOps. Since both these objects tie in closely with circuit, this chapter served as a springboard for future chapters.

8
Building Components for OneOps

In the last chapter, you learned about inductors and circuits. Inductors and circuits form critical components of OneOps and do majority of the work. In this chapter, we will look at various OneOps components. However, before we do that, let's take a step back and do a little recap of what we have seen so far and how it fits in the context of OneOps components.

A brief recap of the OneOps architecture

The OneOps architecture has been covered in detail in the previous chapters. However, when we covered the architecture we did not cover the components, their design, and how they fit in with the overall OneOps scheme. As we have already seen, the front end for OneOps is called **display** and is written in *Ruby On Rails*. Display serves as the front end through which OneOps users can configure clouds, build assemblies, and monitor deployments. OneOps also stores data in three main postgres databases. As described in `Chapter 2`, *Understanding the OneOps Architecture*, everything relevant to OneOps is stored in one of these databases. Besides these, OneOps runs a host of backend services that provide a lot of functionality. These services talk to each other over the ActiveMQ messaging service. Again, as described in detail in `Chapter 2`, *Understanding the OneOps Architecture*, these services act on two types of messages: a work order or an action order. A work order is a request for change that will result in a physical change to a *change item*. This means this will result in an addition or deletion of an item from OneOps. For example, the deployment of an application or the removal of an application occurs via a work order.

An action item is structurally like a work order but does not result in a physical change to a change item. It results only in the change of state of a change item. Examples would be starting, stopping, or restarting a service. These work orders and action orders are acted upon by the inductor. At the most basic level, work orders and action orders act as a wrapper on top of assemblies, which themselves are composed of platforms and components and the interdependencies between them. All change items attached to a work order are processed by the adapter. The adapter provides the REST API for any changes made to models, change items, deployments, and namespaces. As a matter of fact, if you tail the development log available in `/opt/oneops/log/development.log` then you can clearly see all the requests being sent to the adapter.

```
ue&nsPath=%2FOneOps%2Ftest&releaseState=closed
   HTTP Get (6.8ms)  http://cmsapi:8080/adapter/rest/dj/simple/releases?latest=tr
ue&nsPath=%2FOneOps%2Ftest%2Fdev%2Fmanifest
   HTTP Get (8.8ms)  http://cmsapi:8080/adapter/rest/dj/simple/releases?nsPath=%2
FOneOps%2Ftest%2Fdev%2Fbom&releaseState=open
   HTTP Get (58.6ms)  http://cmsapi:8080/adapter/rest/dj/simple/deployments?lates
t=true&nsPath=%2FOneOps%2Ftest%2Fdev%2Fbom
   HTTP Get (29.0ms)  http://cmsapi:8080/adapter/rest/dj/simple/relations?ciId=14
7319&direction=from&relationShortName=ComposedOf&targetClassName=manifest.Platfo
rm
   HTTP Get (15.5ms)  http://cmsapi:8080/adapter/rest/dj/simple/relations?nsPath=
%2FOneOps%2Ftest%2Fdev%2Fmanifest&relationShortName=LinksTo
   HTTP Post (8.8ms)  http://search:9200/cms/release/_search
   HTTP Get (69.4ms)  http://cmsapi:8080/adapter/rest/dj/simple/relations?ciId=14
7319&direction=from&relationName=base.Consumes&targetClassName=account.Cloud
   HTTP Get (17.6ms)  http://cmsapi:8080/adapter/rest/cm/simple/relations?include
ToCi=true&nsPath=%2FOneOps%2Ftest%2Fdev&recursive=true&relationName=base.Consume
s&targetClassName=account.Cloud
   HTTP Get (8.3ms)  http://cmsapi:8080/adapter/rest/cm/simple/relations?nsPath=%
2FOneOps%2Ftest%2Fdev%2Fbom&recursive=true&relationShortName=DeployedTo
   HTTP Get (5.6ms)  http://cmsapi:8080/adapter/rest/cm/simple/cis?ciClassName=ac
count.Environment&nsPath=%2FOneOps
   HTTP Get (8.6ms)  http://cmsapi:8080/adapter/rest/cm/simple/cis?ciClassName=ac
count.Cloud&nsPath=%2FOneOps%2F_clouds
```

What are components?

Components form the most basic building blocks in OneOps. We have had brief encounters with components before in the circuit directory. Here we will deep dive into components. As mentioned in the OneOps documentation, a component has three aspects--a component class, a component resource, and a component instance. This kind of structure will be instantly recognizable to people familiar with the object-oriented style of programming. In object-oriented programming objects are always instantiated from classes. Similarly, the equivalent of a class in OneOps is a component. Just like a class has variables and methods associated with it, so does a component. Since the backend of OneOps is, currently, heavily modeled in Chef, a OneOps component is a Chef cookbook modified to work with OneOps. In the next chapter, you will be creating your own components from scratch. However, before you start creating your components, you should understand their structure. At the time of writing, OneOps uses Chef version 11. A OneOps component uses a modified version of Chef Cookbook. If you look into a `components` directory, you will see directories such as `attributes`, `doc`, `files`, `libraries`, `recipes`, and `templates` as well as the `metadata.rb` and `README.md` file. Each file and directory serves a purpose. At a high level, in a programmatic way, you can think of a component as a class with a unique functionality of the class stored in each of these directories. For example, like a class's variables, the commonly used variables are stored in the attributes directory. Similarly like a classes subroutines, functions or behavior the component's executable parts are stored in the recipes directory. The best way to understand the structure of a component is to look at an existing component and try to understand what it contains. As an example, let's look at the tomcat component. If you go to the directory `/opt/oneops/inductor/circuit-oneops-1/components/cookbooks/tomcat`, you will see multiple files and directories listed there.

```
[root@localhost tomcat]# pwd
/opt/oneops/inductor/circuit-oneops-1/components/cookbooks/tomcat
[root@localhost tomcat]# ls -l
total 32
drwxr-xr-x. 2 root root    23 Feb 25 23:14 attributes
drwxr-xr-x. 2 root root    38 Feb 25 23:14 doc
drwxr-xr-x. 3 root root    38 Feb 25 23:14 files
drwxr-xr-x. 2 root root    20 Feb 25 23:14 libraries
-rw-r--r--. 1 root root 22846 Feb 25 23:14 metadata.rb
-rw-r--r--. 1 root root   782 Feb 25 23:14 README.md
drwxr-xr-x. 2 root root  4096 Feb 25 23:14 recipes
drwxr-xr-x. 3 root root    20 Feb 25 23:14 templates
[root@localhost tomcat]# 
```

Under attributes you will find a file called `default.rb`, which has values for a lot of variables. These variables can be used in multiple locations throughout your recipes. If a change is required to any variable, instead of hunting it down across multiple recipes and changing it, `default.rb` provides a convenient and central location from which to change.

```
# Tomcat
tversion = "tomcat"+node[:tomcat][:version][0,1]
default["tomcat"]["port"] = 8080
default["tomcat"]["server_port"] = 8005
default["tomcat"]["ssl_port"] = 8443
default["tomcat"]["ajp_port"] = 8009
default["tomcat"]["java_options"] = "-Djava.awt.headless=true"
default["tomcat"]["use_security_manager"] = false
default["tomcat"]["webapp_install_dir"] = "/var/lib/#{tversion}/webapps"
default["tomcat"]["stop_time"] = 45
# Default thread pool configuration
default['tomcat']['executor']['executor_name'] = 'tomcatThreadPool'
default['tomcat']['executor']['max_threads'] = '50'
default['tomcat']['executor']['min_spare_threads'] = '25'
# Default TLS Ciphers.
# Note the cipher list is not updated if different TLS versions are enabled/disa
bled. Tomcat chooses the appropriate ciphers from this list based on the TLS ver
sions enabled.
@
@
@
@
@
"default.rb" 64L, 3826C
```

This also makes it an excellent place for you to store any configuration details for your software, if your component deals with software installation. The `doc` folder stores any documentation related to the component especially in the `md` format. It can also contain an image in the `png` format with the name same as the component. If it does, after a CMS sync the image is displayed next to the component in OneOps. Next, in the `files` directory, you can have files that you can copy verbatim to any nodes you want. This can include any configuration or binary files.

```
[root@localhost tomcat]# ls -l
total 32
drwxr-xr-x. 2 root root    23 Mar 15 19:56 attributes
drwxr-xr-x. 2 root root    38 Feb 25 23:14 doc
drwxr-xr-x. 3 root root    38 Feb 25 23:14 files
drwxr-xr-x. 2 root root    20 Feb 25 23:14 libraries
-rw-r--r--. 1 root root 22846 Feb 25 23:14 metadata.rb
-rw-r--r--. 1 root root   782 Feb 25 23:14 README.md
drwxr-xr-x. 2 root root  4096 Feb 25 23:14 recipes
drwxr-xr-x. 3 root root    20 Feb 25 23:14 templates
[root@localhost tomcat]# ls -l files
total 4
-rw-r--r--. 1 root root 688 Feb 25 23:14 context.xml
drwxr-xr-x. 2 root root  24 Feb 25 23:14 default
[root@localhost tomcat]# ls -l files/default/
total 4
-rw-r--r--. 1 root root 782 Feb 25 23:14 ROOT.tar.gz
[root@localhost tomcat]#
```

For people who know Chef this structure will look very familiar. For people who do not know Chef, this will serve as a primer to cookbook structure.

Under `libraries` you will find `library` files created for specific cookbooks. These are libraries that change the functionality of some existing Chef behavior or create a brand-new behavior that is not offered by Chef. This is done by extending an existing `Chef` library or starting a brand-new Chef library. Libraries provide utility functionality that your script might depend on and which can be called multiple times.

```
[root@localhost tomcat]# more libraries/util.rb

def get_attribute_value(attr_name)
        node.workorder.rfcCi.ciBaseAttributes.has_key?(attr_name)? node.workorde
r.rfcCi.ciBaseAttributes[attr_name] : node.tomcat[attr_name]
end

def tom_ver
        case node.tomcat.install_type
        when "repository"
                return "tomcat"
        when "binary"
                return "tomcat"+node[:tomcat][:version][0,1]
        end
end

def exit_with_error(msg)
        Chef::Log.error(msg)
        puts "***FAULT:FATAL=#{msg}"
        Chef::Application.fatal!(msg)
end
[root@localhost tomcat]#
```

The `recipes` directory contains scripts that provide the main functionality for the cookbook. Any components can have multiple recipes. Moreover, a recipe can call another recipe, effectively extending it. It is recommended a recipe should always serve a single purpose such as installing a component, starting, stopping, deleting, and so on. Recipes are also the place from where you will be referring to the configuration that you defined in attributes. In OneOps the recipes do all the heavy lifting in terms of installing and maintaining the components on various instances. If you want to add a custom component to your OneOps, chances are you will have to write custom recipes. Recipes are written in Ruby with the advantage that they have access to the Chef DSL. In OneOps they also have access to all the workorder data as well as all the CI data needed to operate on any given CI.

```
[[root@localhost recipes]# pwd
/opt/oneops/inductor/circuit-oneops-1/components/cookbooks/tomcat/recipes
[[root@localhost recipes]# ls
add_binary.rb   default.rb       restart.rb             update.rb
add.rb          delete.rb        setwrapperattribs.rb   validateAppVersion.rb
add_repo.rb     force-restart.rb start.rb               versionstatus.rb
build.rb        force-stop.rb    status.rb
cleanup.rb      repair.rb        stop.rb
debug.rb        replace.rb       threaddump.rb
[root@localhost recipes]# ▎
```

The `templates` directory is just like files directory; however, it contains files with parameters that can be replaced on-the-fly to generate text files. This is useful to generate things such as configuration files in which values are not known in advance or in which input is provided by user just before installation. People familiar with *Ruby on Rails* will recognize the embedded Ruby files where the Ruby code is replaced on-the-fly by Chef just like Rails does. For instance, of Tomcat installation feedback can be asked from user for the user and group under which to install tomcat and the user and the group can then be replaced on-the-fly in the configuration file. The other contents of the configuration file stay static; hence this file is a good candidate for this directory.

```
#
# Dynamically generated by Chef on <%= node.workorder.rfcCi.ciName %> in namespa
ce <%= node.workorder.rfcCi.nsPath %>
#
# Local modifications will be overwritten by Chef.
#

# Run Tomcat as this user ID. Not setting this or leaving it blank will use the
# default of TOMCAT.
<%
if node["tomcat"].has_key?("tomcat_user") && !node["tomcat"]["tomcat_user"].empt
y?
%>
TOMCAT_USER=<%= node["tomcat"]["tomcat_user"] %>
<%
else
%>
TOMCAT_USER=<%= node["tomcat"]["user"] %>
<%
end
%>

# Run Tomcat as this group ID. Not setting this or leaving it blank will use
"templates/default/default_tomcat.erb" 97L, 3234C
```

Lastly, the cookbook metadata file resides in the root directory of the component cookbook. It is used to store useful information about the component such as version, maintainer, email, and so on. It also stores dependency information; if the component depends on any other components or cookbooks, then those cookbooks and the relevant recipes are executed first. Metadata also contains lots of other useful information such as grouping of CMS models that the component depends on. It also contains attributes that get modeled as GUI components in OneOps.

```
name                    "Tomcat"
description             "Installs/Configures tomcat"
version                 "0.1"
maintainer              "OneOps"
maintainer_email        "support@oneops.com"
license                 "Apache License, Version 2.0"
depends                 "shared"
depends                 "javaservicewrapper"

grouping 'default',
        :access => "global",
        :packages => ['base', 'mgmt.catalog', 'mgmt.manifest', 'catalog', 'mani
fest', 'bom']


# installation attributes
attribute 'install_type',
        :description => "Installation Type",
        :required => "required",
        :default => "repository",
        :format => {
            :category => '1.Global',
@
```

Attributes can also be defined as hardcoded values and not modeled in the GUI if needed.

A look at packs

So far, we have explored the structure of a component that is a very standalone object. Once you have modeled your component, you will have to create a corresponding pack file under the `packs` directory, which resides under the same level as the components directory. The configuration and instructions found in the pack file define several things for a component, including not limited to the following:

- What services and other components it depends on
- Default values for attributes
- Monitor and threshold definitions
- Custom payload details
- Relationships such as `depends_on`, `managed_via`, and `secured_via`

A pack also defines the order of execution of components and is used to string components together to make them more effective and reusable.

```
  :from_resource => 'tomcat-daemon',
  :to_resource => 'keystore',
  :attributes => {"propagate_to" => "from", "flex" => false, "min" => 1, "max" =
> 1}

relation "keystore::depends_on::certificate",
  :relation_name => 'DependsOn',
  :from_resource => 'keystore',
  :to_resource => 'certificate',
  :attributes => {"propagate_to" => "from", "flex" => false, "min" => 1, "max" =
> 1}


# managed_via
[ 'tomcat', 'artifact', 'build', 'java','keystore', 'tomcat-daemon'].each do |fr
om|
  relation "#{from}::managed_via::compute",
    :except => [ '_default' ],
    :relation_name => 'ManagedVia',
    :from_resource => from,
    :to_resource    => 'compute',
    :attributes     => { }
end
"tomcat.rb" line 295 of 295 --100%-- col 1
```

Once a pack is defined it can be synced with the CMS using the included `knife` command or the OneOps CLI.

A look at platforms

A component, along together its pack file, makes a platform. A platform consists of everything needed to install the component including the dependencies, the backend scripts, the data required install and monitor the component, including the information required for repairing and scaling it. This pairing of a component and pack to make a platform is created after the CMS sync.

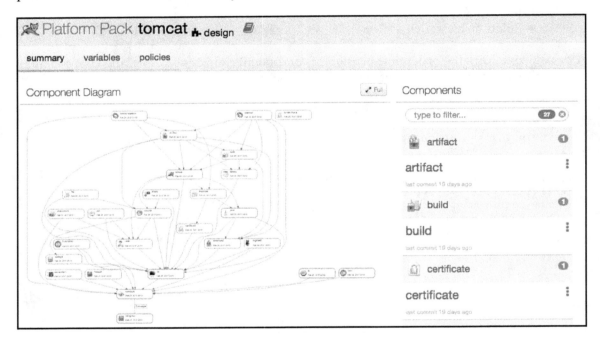

What are assemblies?

So far, we have created assemblies and even transitioned assemblies to various environments and managed them. Now that we know the structure of the components that make up assemblies, we can look more closely at how assemblies themselves are structured. As we know an assembly goes through three phases: **design, transition**, and **operation**. In the design phase the assembly does not contain any environment details nor does it contain any operational components. At CMS level the components extend a class called **catalog**, which in turn extends a class called **base**. In transition phase two, additional components get added to the assembly IaaS object, such as a load balancer or DNS. These can also be specific to a cloud provider. The second object added to the assembly at this point is monitors. Transition relationships in an assembly are denoted by the class manifest. The last phase an assembly goes through is operation. In the operation phase, corresponding **Bill Of Material** (**BOM**) components are created for each component in an assembly for which a manifest component exists. This creates a binding between the components in the assembly and the cloud on which they are deployed, which in turn creates a physical link between the component and the cloud and translates the assembly to the cloud infrastructure and deployment.

Summary

In this chapter, we explored the theory behind components, packs, platforms, and assemblies. We also provided a detailed explanation of each component part and its utility. In the next chapter, we will create a custom OneOps component from scratch and add it to our system.

9

Adding and Managing OneOps Components

Last chapter served to give you a detailed understanding of components, platforms, assemblies and how they depend on each other. That detailed exploration will help you to create complex components that are interdependent and linked to create complex deployments that are reusable. This will allow you to unlock the true power of OneOps. In this chapter, we will take a very practical look at OneOps. We will create a component from scratch. We will follow all the steps from inception to deployment and monitoring to demonstrate how new components can be added to OneOps, how they can be made part of an assembly and how they can be monitored effectively after deployment.

Planning your component

Essentially to add your component to OneOps you will be writing a Chef cookbook that will support the component. If a Chef cookbook already exists for the software that you are trying to add support for then you will save a lot of time. However, you will still need to make changes to the cookbook to make it compliant with OneOps. If a cookbook does not exist for the software that you are trying to add then you will have to create one by hand. The easiest way to do so is to copy an existing cookbook and then edit it for your needs. Chef is very robust and mature software and has cookbooks available for almost all your software needs. In this chapter, we will be creating a cookbook in detail for software for which a Chef cookbook already exists. We will be creating all OneOps parts from scratch instead of copying and editing existing ones. This will help us understand the nitty gritty and plumbing of the backend.

Irrespective of the software you want to install, there are a few things you should consider before you start writing or editing your cookbook as this will affect the choices you make:

- What actions are required by your software and what actions will your recipes provide? Most standard software has start, stop, and restart. OneOps allows a repair option. Will you provide any other options?
- What are the dependencies and prerequisites for your software? Does it need Java, Ruby, Python, or any other libraries installed to function properly? Is it dependent on any version?
- How configurable is your install? What options will you be asking from the user? The installation directory? Memory options for Java?
- Will you be installing from binary? RPM or compiling from source? Will that be provided as a selectable option?
- Does your software need to start itself when the OS starts via `init.d` or upstart?
- Does it have any other special requirements such as being added to Cron, running scripts, and so on?

Once you start asking these questions and more in the context of your software and start listing the answers, you will understand how your cookbook should function.

Adding a new component

For this book, we will be adding a brand-new component to OneOps, one that did not exist before. This way you, as a developer, can see all the steps needed to successfully add a new component to OneOps. We will be adding a database called **OrientDB**. OrientDB is a multimodal database that primary functions as a graph database. This means it can function as a graph database as well as a document database depending on the need. You can read more on these features at `http://orientdb.com/multi-model_database/`. Feature-wise, OrientDB is very much like MongoDB or Neo4J. However, you can choose to add any software as a component. The reason we choose OrientDB is because it has all the hallmarks of a typical server. It can be added as a service. It has configurable ports. It has start and stop scripts; and it has dependency on Java. This will serve well to demonstrate various aspects and steps needed to add a component. So, let's start with generating the necessary files for our new component.

Login to your OneOps instance as root user and go to your default `circuit` directory. As mentioned in the previous chapter, a component is a cookbook supported by a host of recipes and defined by its metadata. In OneOps speak it's called a **model**. You can operate on models by issuing the command `knife model` followed by the appropriate options. Use the following command to generate the required files for the OrientDB component.

```
knife model create orientdb
```

This will generate a model called `orientdb` under the `component/cookbooks` directory.

```
[root@ip-172-31-52-21 circuit-oneops-1]# knife model create orientdb
** Creating cookbook orientdb
/home/oneops/build/circuit-oneops-1/components/cookbooks : orientdb
** Creating README for cookbook: orientdb
** Creating CHANGELOG for cookbook: orientdb
[root@ip-172-31-52-21 circuit-oneops-1]# ls components/cookbooks/orientdb/
attributes     definitions  libraries    providers   recipes      templates
CHANGELOG.md   files        metadata.rb  README.md   resources
[root@ip-172-31-52-21 circuit-oneops-1]# 
```

This generates entirely too many files. However, this also prevents us from creating the structure by hand and does most of the heavy work for us. As you can see in the preceding screenshot it creates the skeleton of a Chef cookbook for us called `orientdb`.

We can start by editing the file `metadata.rb`. `metadata.rb` holds lots of useful information about the component including its name, description, version, and maintainer. It also holds various attributes for our components.

```
grouping 'default',
  :access => 'global',
  :packages => ['base', 'mgmt.catalog', 'mgmt.manifest', 'catalog', 'manifest','
bom']

attribute 'version',
  :description => 'Version',
  :required => 'required',
  :default => '2.2.16',
  :format => {
    :help => 'Version of OrientDB',
    :category => '1.Global',
    :order => 1,
    :form => { 'field' => 'select', 'options_for_select' => [['2.2.16','2.2.16']
,['2.2.15','2.2.15']] }
  }

recipe "status", "orientdb Status"
recipe "start", "orientdb Start"
recipe "stop", "orientdb Stop"
recipe "restart", "orientdb Restart"
recipe "repair", "orientdb Repair"
```

However, as seen in the preceding screenshot, we are going to make some changes to the metadata file to suit our needs. Firstly, we change the name, description, and maintainer information to match what is correct. In this instance, I changed the name and description to OrientDB. Then notice in the grouping under packages we added a package called `bom` which stands for **Bill of Materials**. If you recall, during the transition and operation phase `bom` components are created for all manifest components with relationships to all the clouds to which they are deployed. Hence having a reference to the `bom` package is important. Next, for now, we will add only a single attribute called `Version`. This will allow us to choose what version of OrientDB to install. We have set the default version to 2.2.16, which, as of this writing, is the latest version. Since we want this attribute to show up as a selectable option on the GUI, we supply it with a form option and make it a `select` field. `options_for_select` is a multi-dimensional array or what is called as *array of arrays*. It contains a set of elements each with similar-looking options. The first is how the name will look like in the selection box and the second is the actual value of the variable to which it will be assigned.

In most cases, it is simple to keep both the values the same. Here we are providing the latest version and the previous version as the versions available for installation. Later, if we choose to make the installation more interactive by providing more options, we can add more attributes here. We may choose to add attributes for the default installation directory, the user under which the software will get installed, and perhaps options that get passed to JVM. Not all options need to have a corresponding editable field in the GUI forms. Lastly, we change the names of the recipes to what OneOps expects and will call by default, namely status, start, stop, restart, and repair. These recipes will also show up as action buttons with the appropriate descriptions in the operations phase when you transition your component from design in the OneOps GUI. However, as you can see under the recipes directory, none of these recipes exist.

```
#
# Cookbook Name:: orientdb
# Recipe:: add.rb
#
# Copyright 2017, YOUR_COMPANY_NAME
#
~
~
~
~
~
~
~
~
~
~
~
~
~
~
~
"add.rb" 8L, 135C
```

Moreover, all the recipes are empty. This means we will have to write each recipe manually by hand. Thankfully, as mentioned before, Chef is robust and mature software and has recipes for pretty much everything.

A grouping of related Chef recipes is called a cookbook. Cookbooks for pretty much anything can be found in the Chef supermarket, which is located at `https://supermarket.chef.io/`. Before you write your own cookbook you should search the supermarket and if, one exists, you should download it.

A quick search of Chef supermarket reveals that there already exists a cookbook for `orientdb`, saving us the trouble of writing one from scratch. The relevant cookbook can be found at `https://supermarket.chef.io/cookbooks/orientdb`. Let's download the code for the cookbook with the following command:

```
git clone https://github.com/fgimenez/orientdb-cookbook.git
```

 Run the `git clone` command in a different directory than your components directory. Running it in `/tmp` is fine.

You can get to the `git` repository by clicking the **View Source** button on the right side of the page on the Chef supermarket. Once your download the cookbook, you will see that the cookbook has similar structure to what you have already created. Particularly we are interested in the three attributes, recipes, and templates directories.

```
[root@ip-172-31-52-21 ~]# git clone https://github.com/fgimenez/orientdb-cookboo
k.git
Cloning into 'orientdb-cookbook'...
remote: Counting objects: 364, done.
remote: Total 364 (delta 0), reused 0 (delta 0), pack-reused 364
Receiving objects: 100% (364/364), 63.70 KiB | 0 bytes/s, done.
Resolving deltas: 100% (190/190), done.
[root@ip-172-31-52-21 ~]# ls orientdb-cookbook/
attributes  bootstrap.sh  metadata.rb  README.md  spec       test
Berksfile   Gemfile       Rakefile     recipes    templates  Vagrantfile
[root@ip-172-31-52-21 ~]#
```

We need to copy files from each of these directories to the corresponding directory in our cookbook. This will help us avoid lots of manual coding. You can use the commands following to copy the files over.

```
cd orientdb-cookbook/
cp -pr attributes/* /opt/oneops/inductor/circuit-oneops-1/components/
cookbooks/orientdb/attributes/
cp -pr recipes/* /opt/oneops/inductor/circuit-oneops-1/components/
cookbooks/orientdb/recipes/
```

```
cp -pr templates/* /opt/oneops/inductor/circuit-oneops-1/components/
cookbooks/orientdb/templates/
```

The file in directories `attribute` folder, called `default.rb`, provides default values for a lot of variables. Theses values can be overridden inside the recipes. The files under the templates directory provide templates for various configuration files with replaceable parameters. These files will be used to configure the server during deployment. Finally, the recipes provide many useful functions to download, install, stop, and start the server. For `orientdb` you will see these are provided by a bunch of recipes that are all called from the default recipe. Since we want to provide different functions such as `start`, `stop`, `restart`, `repair` , and so on, for now we will be just calling the default recipe from these recipes. Later as need arises we can modify these recipes to provide more specific functions.

```
[root@ip-172-31-52-21 recipes]# pwd
/opt/oneops/inductor/circuit-oneops-1/components/cookbooks/orientdb/recipes
[root@ip-172-31-52-21 recipes]# more add.rb

  #
  # Cookbook Name:: orientdb
  # Recipe:: add.rb
  #
  # Copyright 2017, YOUR_COMPANY_NAME
  #
include_recipe 'orientdb::default'
[root@ip-172-31-52-21 recipes]# more status.rb

  #
  # Cookbook Name:: orientdb
  # Recipe:: status.rb
  #
  # Copyright 2017, YOUR_COMPANY_NAME
  #
include_recipe "orientdb::default"
[root@ip-172-31-52-21 recipes]#
```

At this point we can upload the cookbook to the CMS and clear the cache using the following commands:

```
[root@ip-172-31-52-21 circuit-oneops-1]# knife model sync orientdb
Processing metadata for orientdb from /home/oneops/build/circuit-oneops-1/compone
nts/cookbooks/orientdb/metadata.rb
Updating class base.oneops.1.Orientdb
Successfuly saved class base.oneops.1.Orientdb
Updating class mgmt.catalog.oneops.1.Orientdb
Successfuly saved class mgmt.catalog.oneops.1.Orientdb
Updating class mgmt.manifest.oneops.1.Orientdb
Successfuly saved class mgmt.manifest.oneops.1.Orientdb
Updating class catalog.oneops.1.Orientdb
Successfuly saved class catalog.oneops.1.Orientdb
Updating class manifest.oneops.1.Orientdb
Successfuly saved class manifest.oneops.1.Orientdb
Updating class bom.oneops.1.Orientdb
Successfuly saved class bom.oneops.1.Orientdb
remote_dir:
   <Fog::Storage::Local::Directory
    key="cms"
  >
package_name: mgmt.catalog
package_name: mgmt.manifest
package_name: catalog
package_name: manifest
package_name: bom
[root@ip-172-31-52-21 circuit-oneops-1]#
```

This syncs the component and its associated recipes with the CMS. Now OneOps is fully aware of our OrientDB component. As a matter of fact, you can use cms-admin, mentioned in Chapter 1, *Getting Started with OneOps,* to browse to the following URL to confirm that OrientDB shows up in CMS:

```
http://<your OneOps Server>:8080/cms-
admin/md.do?type=clazz&name=base.oneops.1.Orientdb
```

Class Definition Detail

base.oneops.1.Orientdb

Short Class Name:	Orientdb
Access Level:	global
Implementation:	oo::chef-11.18.12
Is Namespace:	false
Use class name in ns:	false
Description:	Installs/Configures orientdb
Created:	Mon Feb 20 20:54:16 UTC 2017

However, if you create a test assembly and try to add OrientDB to it, it does not show up in the list of available components.

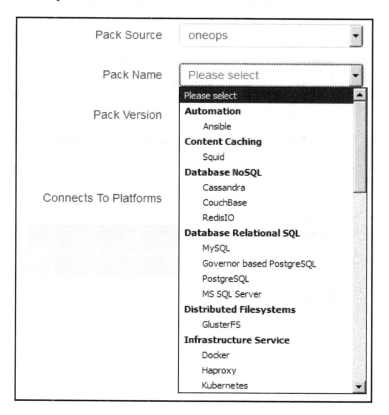

So, what gives? Our component is ready and we followed all the steps correctly. Our component should have shown up as an available component in the list. Clearly, we missed something. The answer is on the page on which we have trying to add the component. It is asking us to add a platform and we are yet to define `orientdb` as a platform.

Creating a new platform

As we saw in the previous chapter, a platform is a single component or a collection of components grouped together for reusability. A platform not only defines what the component is and where it belongs but also its dependencies and relationships to other components. Platforms also allow components to be grouped together via inheritance, dependencies, or other methods to create a pack so that an appropriate software state is maintained. So, let's look at our component and see how we can turn it into a platform.

We start by going to the directory called packs under our default `circuit`. Under that directory, you will notice there are already files for all the applications that are currently available as platforms under OneOps.

```
[[root@ip-172-31-52-21 packs]# ls
activemq.rb            es.rb               kibana.rb              puppetexample.rb
ansible.rb             flamegraph.rb       kubernetes-app.rb      python.rb
apache.rb              genericdb.rb        kubernetes.rb          rabbitmq.rb
base.rb                genericlb.rb        lbdb.rb                rails-nginx.rb
cassandra.rb           genericmq.rb        mssql.rb               rails.rb
cluster.rb             generic_ring.rb     mysql.rb               redisio.rb
containerizedlb.rb     glusterfs.rb        nfs.rb                 ruby.rb
containerized.rb       go.rb               nginx.rb               solrcloud.rb
couchbase.rb           graphite.rb         nodejs.rb              squid.rb
customlb.rb            haproxy.rb          node.rb                tomcat-2.rb
custom.rb              iis.rb              php.rb                 tomcat.rb
doc                    inductor.rb         play.rb                zookeeper.rb
docker.rb              javalb.rb           postgresql-governor.rb
dotnet-framework.rb    java.rb             postgresql.rb
dotnet.rb              jboss.rb            powerdns.rb
[root@ip-172-31-52-21 packs]# 
```

Each file defines the type of component, its description, its category, the resources it offers, and its dependencies. We start by creating a brand-new file here called `orientdb.rb`. The very first thing we will add to it is extending the generic ring pack. Since OrientDB is a NoSQL database, like other NoSQL databases such as Cassandra and Redis, OrientDB will be including the pack provided by OneOps called the generic ring pack. We will then provide other basic information in the file such as the name, description, type, and the category of the platform. In our case the name and the description are `"orientdb"`, the type is `"Platform"` and the category is `"Database NoSQL"`. The category is the grouping under the `Pack Name` menu where our platform will show up while designing our assembly.

```
include_pack "generic_ring"
[]
name "orientdb"
description "OrientDB"
type "Platform"
category "Database NoSQL"
~
~
~
~
~
~
~
~
~
~
~
~
~
~
~
~
~
"orientdb.rb" 6L, 110C
```

These are the bare-bones details needed for our component to show up as a platform in OneOps. However, for our component to be more functional we will need to add more functionality and detail. So now let's take it a step further by adding OrientDB as a resource. We add the cookbook that we created as a cookbook in the platform. Notice we use the class name of the cookbook and not the actual name. We also add `secgroup` as a resource. We leave port 22 and all the ports above 1024 open for now. Of course, we can look up the exact ports used by OrientDB and tighten up our security and open only specific ports, which is highly recommended. But for our tutorial this should suffice for now.

```
include_pack "generic_ring"

name "orientdb"
description "OrientDB"
type "Platform"
category "Database NoSQL"

resource "orientdb",
        :cookbook => "oneops.1.orientdb",
        :design => true,
        :requires => {"constraint" => "1..1" }

resource "secgroup",
        :cookbook => "oneops.1.secgroup",
        :design => true,
        :attributes => {
                "inbound" => '[ "22 22 tcp 0.0.0.0/0", "1024 65535 tcp 0.0.0.0/0
" ]'
        },
        :requires => {
                :constraint => "1..1",
                :services => "compute"
        }
"orientdb.rb" 23L, 463C written
```

With this in place we are now ready to upload and sync our pack with the CMS and see the results. The following commands will sync the pack from the circuit directory.

```
Knife pack sync orientdb -reload
```

As the command runs you will notice that the pack now syncs with CMS and all the relevant data is uploaded.

```
Updating monitor ssh for compute in mgmt.manifest
Successfuly saved monitor ssh for compute in mgmt.manifest
Updating monitor cpu for os in mgmt.manifest
Successfuly saved monitor cpu for os in mgmt.manifest
Updating monitor load for os in mgmt.manifest
Successfuly saved monitor load for os in mgmt.manifest
Updating monitor disk for os in mgmt.manifest
Successfuly saved monitor disk for os in mgmt.manifest
Updating monitor mem for os in mgmt.manifest
Successfuly saved monitor mem for os in mgmt.manifest
Updating monitor network for os in mgmt.manifest
Successfuly saved monitor network for os in mgmt.manifest
Updating monitor logstashprocess for logstash in mgmt.manifest
Successfuly saved monitor logstashprocess for logstash in mgmt.manifest
Updating monitor usage for volume in mgmt.manifest
Successfuly saved monitor usage for volume in mgmt.manifest
Updating monitor process for daemon in mgmt.manifest
Successfuly saved monitor process for daemon in mgmt.manifest
Updating monitor ExpiryMetrics for certificate in mgmt.manifest
Successfuly saved monitor ExpiryMetrics for certificate in mgmt.manifest
Uploaded pack orientdb
Updating pack orientdb
Updating pack orientdb version 1
Successfuly saved pack orientdb version 1
[root@ip-172-31-52-21 circuit-oneops-1]#
```

We can now login to our OneOps instance, create an assembly, and add the OrientDB platform to it. If you do so, you will immediately notice a couple of problems with it.

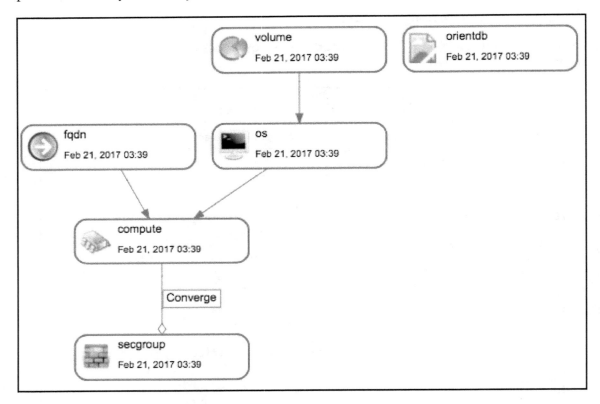

Firstly, OrientDB shows up standalone with no dependencies at all on anything, which is not good. Secondly, the icon for OrientDB shows up as a broken folder, which does not look pretty. The second problem is easily fixed. Under the packs directory you will find a directory called `doc`. In this directory, you will already see PNG files corresponding to existing software. Download an appropriate logo or image for the software that you are adding and copy it to this directory. Be sure to call it with your software name. In our case, it is `orientdb.png`. Also under the cookbook directory that we created for OrientDB create a directory called **doc**. Copy the same file under this directory. You will have to name carefully.

The name will have to be same as the name of the cookbook. Probably, it will be same name as your software with the first letter as a capital. In our case, it is `Orientdb.png`. Once done reload the model and the pack by issuing the commands following.

```
Knife model sync orientdb
Knife pack sync orientdb -reload
```

Now reload the design screen again and you will see that OrientDB logo shows up nicely next to our platform. Now let's add a few more details to the pack. We will add Java as a dependency since OrientDB depends on Java. Next, we will also add relationships between various components as follows.

```
                        :version => '7'
            }

#depends_on
[ { :from => 'orientdb', :to => 'os' },
  { :from => 'orientdb', :to => 'java'},
  { :from => 'java', :to => 'os'}, ].each do |link|
        relation "#{link[:from]}::depends_on::{link[:to]}",
        :relation_name => 'DependsOn',
        :from_resource => link[:from],
        :to_resource => link[:to],
        :attributes => { "flex" => false, "min" => 1, "max" => 1 }
end

#managed_via
['orientdb','java'].each do |from|
        relation "#{from}::managed_via::compute",
                :except => ['_default' ],
                :relation_name => 'ManagedVia',
                :from_resource => from,
                :to_resource => 'compute',
                :attributes => {}
end
"orientdb.rb" 55L, 1278C written
```

As you can see we have added the two types of relationship that are required by OneOps, namely **DependsOn** and **ManagedVia**. Specifically, here we are saying that OrientDB and Java depend on OS. Also, OrientDB depends on Java. The syntax here is important since all the links are defined as an array and we are simply defining a loop that is being cycled through. Similarly, in the ManagedVia section we are saying that OriendDB and Java are managed via the compute instance. This makes sense since both are deployed on top of the compute instance. Now sync up the pack again and make a brand-new assembly; this time you will see that the results are very different indeed.

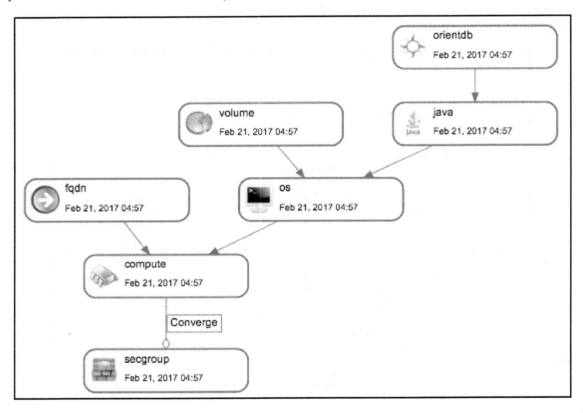

You can see now the logo is showing up properly. OrientDB shows up as dependent on Java, which is in turn dependent on the OS.

Installing and testing the new component

Now that the new platform is showing up in the design phase, we can test it out by deploying it. To test it out you must have a cloud configured. By now you should have at least a test OneOps system configured for all your development and testing needs. Configuring a cloud should also be easy for you. So go ahead and create a test assembly. Add the freshly created OrientDB platform to it. When you are deploying a newly created platform for the first time, you should fully expect it to fail. It is rare that things will go right the first time. This is the reason you should be doing this in a test or development environment.

 Another reason to test in a development environment is that you can test with the latest and greatest code, that is, the master branch. That will ensure your code is compatible with the latest changes that OneOps will release. Since OneOps is an Open Source project you should also check in your changes to GitHub and file pull requests to release changes in the wild once they are sufficiently tested.

Now that we have created a test assembly and added a test environment, we can attempt a deployment. As expected the deployment fails with errors. We see that the deployment failed because the cookbook that we download, specifically `orientdb`, depends on two other cookbooks called `tar` and `apt`, which are not provided by default by OneOps. Somehow, we are going to have to add them to our OneOps system. Adding these may seem simple but as we will soon find out it can be tricky. Our first step is to visit the marketplace again and search it for the relevant cookbooks: `apt` and `tar`. Sure enough you can find these on the marketplace. However, there is an easier way to download and install these. In a place that is convenient but out of the way use the commands given below to download the cookbooks. I download them in `/root` for convenience, although that is not really a recommended place.

```
knife cookbook site download apt
knife cookbook site download tar
```

This will download the latest version of the cookbooks. After you have downloaded the cookbooks, copy them over to your cookbooks directory.

```
cp -pr /root/apt /opt/oneops/inductor/circuit-
oneops-1/components/cookbooks/
cp -pr /root/tar /opt/oneops/inductor/circuit-
oneops-1/components/cookbooks/
```

After the cookbooks are copied over, you will need to add them as dependencies to the `metadata.rb` in `orientdb` cookbook.

```
name 'Orientdb'
maintainer 'OneOps'
maintainer_email 'support@oneops.com'
license 'Apache'
description 'Installs/Configures orientdb'
long_description IO.read(File.join(File.dirname(__FILE__), 'README.md'))
version '0.1'
depends 'apt'
depends 'tar'

grouping 'default',
  :access => 'global',
  :packages => ['base', 'mgmt.catalog', 'mgmt.manifest', 'catalog', 'manifest','b
om']

attribute 'version',
  :description => 'Version',
  :required => 'required',
  :default => '2.2.16',
  :format => {
    :help => 'Version of OrientDB',
    :category => '1.Global',
    :order => 1,
"metadata.rb" 31L, 881C
```

The reason we should add these as dependencies is because, when OrientDB gets installed after the compute and OS runs, OneOps installs Chef on the compute instance; it then copies the cookbook over to the compute instance and runs it. As such, when our cookbooks run Chef does not have all the cookbooks that are installed on the OneOps server readily available to it. As such any cookbooks that are required must be explicitly defined as dependencies so that the Chef server can bundle them and send them over to the client side to run whenever they are needed.

However, even after adding the dependencies and re-running the deployment, you will notice again that you are getting errors. So now this time a little troubleshooting will show you that the latest cookbooks you downloaded require Chef version 12 and above whereas OneOps, at the time of writing, supports Chef version 11.18.12. This means we will have to download and install slightly older revisions of the cookbooks. A little digging on Chef supermarket yields the correct revisions of cookbooks, which for `apt` is `3.0.0` and for `tar` is `1.1.0`. Again, using the previous commands, we download the correct revisions of the cookbooks and install them in the proper place.

```
cd /root
knife cookbook site download apt 3.0.0
knife cookbook site download tar 1.1.0
cp -pr /root/apt /opt/oneops/inductor/circuit-
oneops-1/components/cookbooks/
cp -pr /root/tar /opt/oneops/inductor/circuit-
oneops-1/components/cookbooks/
```

Now that we have copied the cookbooks into their proper place, we can lock the versions into `orientdb metadata.rb`.

```
name 'Orientdb'
maintainer 'OneOps'
maintainer_email 'support@oneops.com'
license 'Apache'
description 'Installs/Configures orientdb'
long_description IO.read(File.join(File.dirname(__FILE__), 'README.md'))
version '0.1'
depends 'apt', '= 3.0.0'
depends 'tar', '= 1.1.0'

grouping 'default',
  :access => 'global',
  :packages => ['base', 'mgmt.catalog', 'mgmt.manifest', 'catalog', 'manifest','b
om']


attribute 'version',
  :description => 'Version',
  :required => 'required',
  :default => '2.2.16',
  :format => {
    :help => 'Version of OrientDB',
    :category => '1.Global',
    :order => 1,
"metadata.rb" 31L, 881C
```

Once all these changes are in place you are now ready to test your deployment again. This time your chances of success are very high.

> It is always a good idea to lock your dependencies to a version. This prevents your cookbooks from breaking or accidentally updating.

Now if you attempt an installation, you will see that the installation succeeds.

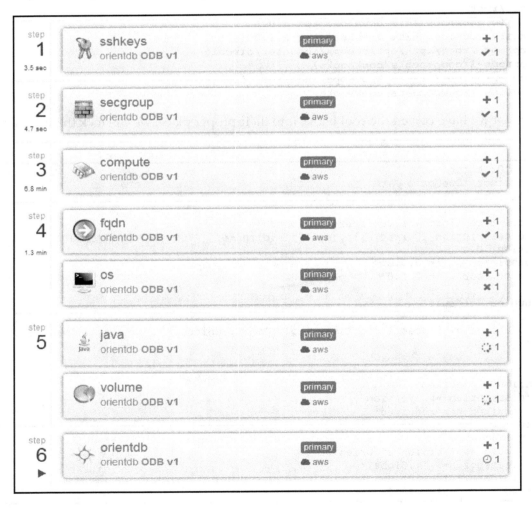

So, to quickly recap, to successfully add a component, we carried out the following steps:

- We created a cookbook for the component.
- We added metadata for the component, which showed up in OneOps GUI.
- We downloaded and added the cookbook for our component and the required recipes. We simply reused the available recipes. If need be we would have written new code.
- We then tested deployments, which produced dependencies for us; these were added to `metadata.rb`.
- Success.

You can access OrientDB Studio at your compute instance address on port `2480`.

Pack maintenance

Now that we have created a brand-new component and a pack, we must maintain them. In general, there are various things we can do to maintain our new pack (and existing packs) in OneOps, such as adding extra attributes, disabling the pack, setting policies and so on. As mentioned earlier we can add extra attributes to metadata.rb to get more input from users and make the installation more interactive. A good guideline is to look at the default.rb file in the attributes directory. This file provides the default value for a lot of variables that are not explicitly supplied when we construct our assembly.

```
default['orientdb']['user']['id'] = 'orientdb'

default['orientdb']['version'] = '2.0.3'
default['orientdb']['flavour'] = 'community'

default['orientdb']['base_tarball_url'] = 'http://www.orientechnologies.com/downl
oad.php?email=unknown@unknown.com&os=linux&file=orientdb'

default['orientdb']['installation_directory'] = "/opt/orientdb"

default['orientdb']['default_init_script'] = "#{default['orientdb']['installation
_directory']}/bin/orientdb.sh"
default['orientdb']['init_script'] = "/etc/init.d/orientdb"

default['orientdb']['db_user'] = 'admin'
default['orientdb']['db_password'] = 'admin'

default['orientdb']['hazelcast']['nodeName'] = node.name
default['orientdb']['hazelcast']['enabled'] = true
default['orientdb']['hazelcast']['group']['name'] = 'orientdb'
default['orientdb']['hazelcast']['group']['password'] = 'orientdb'
default['orientdb']['hazelcast']['network']['port'] = '2434'

default['orientbd']['hazelcast']['network']['join']['mode'] = 'multicast'
"default.rb" 57L, 2661C
```

As you can see, we can very well offer the installation directory as well as db_user and db_password as input fields to the user, thus allowing them more control over the installation. You have two ways of disabling a pack. One is by setting the option ignore to true or false in the pack. If set to true the pack is not reloaded or updated in OneOps. The second way is using enabled. If this is set to false then this pack is not visible to a user while creating a platform or assembly. You can also set policies on your pack. This allows you to conditionally process, restrict, or flag certain things in OneOps and is a very powerful feature. To successfully implement policies though you must know a little bit about the Elasticsearch query language. In general, policies can be applied in two modes, active and passive. The idea is that all objects passing through OneOps are checked against the policies defined in OneOps and, depending on the configuration, the appropriate action is taken. If the policy is enforced in an active mode and the object fails the policy, then the object is not saved in OneOps. However, if the policy is enforced in passive mode and an object fails the policy, the object is saved but marked as failed policy so it can be recognized and reviewed as such. For example, the following policy is taken directly from the OneOps documentation and its explanation:

```
policy "compute-ostype",
        :description => 'custom pack policy for compute-ostype',
        :query => 'ciClassName:(catalog.*Compute manifest.
                    *Compute bom.*Compute) AND NOT ciAttributes.ostype:
                    ("centos-6.5" OR "centos-6.6" OR "redhat-6.5" OR
                    "redhat-6.6" OR "default-cloud")'
        :docUrl => '<document url link for the policy>'`
        :mode => 'active'
```

The above policy is called compute-ostype. It provides a short description. You can also provide a URL to a more descriptive help page in the docUrl parameter. You will also notice that the mode is active. Which means that, if an object fails this policy, it will not be saved. Finally the query, which is written as an Elasticsearch query, essentially says that, during the design phase (catalog.*Compute), the transition phase (manifest.*Compute), or the operation phase (bom.*Compute) "centos-6.6", "redhat-6.5", "redhat-6.6" or "default-cloud" are not allowed. Similar active and passive policies can be defined directly in the pack.

Updating CMS

A cookbook or a pack both need to be synced with the CMS. In `Chapter 2`, *Understanding the OneOps Architecture*, we looked at cms-admin, which allowed us to browse the classes that the CMS stores in the backend. When a pack or a cookbook, or a model as it is known in OneOps context, syncs with CMS, it generates a class for it, maps its dependencies, and performs various other functions that aid it in backend tasks. The various commands to sync with CMS are covered throughout the book. However below is a quick recap of all the commands to sync models and packs with CMS.

```
knife model sync -a # command to sync all models.
Will sync only changed models
knife model sync -a -r # command to sync relations only
knife model sync modelname # command to sync a particular model
knife pack sync -a # command to sync all packs
knife pack sync packname # command to sync a particular pack
knife cloud sync -a # command to sync a particular cloud
knife cloud sync cloudname # command to sync a particular cloud
```

Adding monitoring

Now that we have a fully functioning pack, we can add monitoring to it. Monitoring in OneOps is handled by Nagios, which is an industry standard monitoring tool. Fortunately, Nagios also comes with many utility scripts and monitors preinstalled so we can readily use them instead of reinventing the wheel. These scripts can generally be found in the `/opt/Nagios/libexec` directory. So, if we want to add monitoring to the pack that we just added, all we have to do is to use the Java log file monitoring from Nagios, which comes built in. Since OrientDB is Java-based it works out well for us. All we must do is add the code below to `orientdb.rb` in the `packs` directory.

```
monitors => {
    'Log' => {:description => 'Log',
             :source => '',
             :chart => {'min' => 0, 'unit' => ''},
             :cmd =>
             'check_logfiles!logorientdb!#{cmd_options[:logfile]}!
             #{cmd_options[:warningpattern]}!#{cmd_options
             [:criticalpattern]}',
             :cmd_line => '/opt/nagios/libexec/check_logfiles
             --noprotocol --tag=$ARG1$ --logfile=$ARG2$
             --warningpattern="$ARG3$" --criticalpattern="$ARG4$"',
             :cmd_options => {
                     'logfile' => ' /opt/orientdb/log/
```

```
                        orient-server.log.0',
                        'warningpattern' => 'WARNING',
                        'criticalpattern' => 'CRITICAL'
                        }, :metrics => {
                        'logorientdb_lines' => metric(:unit => 'lines',
                        :description => 'Scanned Lines',
                        :dstype => 'GAUGE'),
                        'logorientdb_warnings' => metric(:
                        'warnings',
                        :description => 'Warnings', :dstype =>
                        'GAUGE'),
                        'logorientdb_criticals' => metric(:unit =>
                        'criticals',
                        :description => 'Criticals', :dstype =>
                        'GAUGE'),
                        'logorientdb_unknowns' => metric(:unit =>
                        'unknowns',
                        :description => 'Unknowns', :dstype => 'GAUGE')
                }, :thresholds => {
                'CriticalLogException' => threshold('15m', 'avg',
                'logorientdb_criticals', trigger('>=', 1, 15, 1),
                reset('<', 1, 15, 1)),
        }
    },
}
```

This will add monitoring to OrientDB log files. All critical, non-critical, and warning messages will show up as gauges in the OneOps GUI in an easily identifiable and understandable visual representation.

Summary

In this chapter, we saw how to add a new component. We then saw how to change the component into a pack by deriving from existing components, adding dependencies, adding dependent code to it, and adding brand-new functionality. We also added peripheral functions to our pack such as policies and monitoring. In the next chapter we will see how to add a custom cloud to OneOps.

10
Adding Your Own Cloud to OneOps

In the previous chapter, you got familiar with custom components, packs, and platforms in OneOps. We also saw how to add custom monitoring to packs. This gave us a good idea of the structure of components and how to write and configure them. In this chapter, we will see how to add a brand new cloud to OneOps. At the time of writing this, OneOps officially supports OpenStack, Rackspace, Microsoft Azure, Amazon AWS, and Google Cloud with support for Alibaba Cloud recently added. However, there are many public and private clouds out there that are not currently supported. Sometimes, you want to deploy your infrastructure to a cloud that is not officially supported by OneOps. Other times your infrastructure may already exist on a cloud unsupported by OneOps. In cases like these, you need not migrate everything to a supported cloud. As you will see, adding a support for a cloud is easy and can be done with minimal effort.

Things to consider when adding support for a cloud

In OneOps Clouds, components, packs, and their corresponding cookbooks are stored under the circuit. We already saw the structure of circuit in `Chapter 7`, *Working with Functional Components*. To quickly recap the definition of clouds and the services that it offers is stored in the directory clouds. The directory `components/cookbooks` stores cookbooks for various components that the cloud will use. The various places from where a cloud will pull data, definitions, cookbooks, and recipes can be quite diverse as we will soon see.

```
[root@ip-172-31-52-21 circuit-oneops-1]# pwd
/opt/oneops/inductor/circuit-oneops-1
[root@ip-172-31-52-21 circuit-oneops-1]# ls -l
total 32
drwxr-xr-x. 2 root root 4096 Sep 29 21:15 catalogs
-rw-r--r--. 1 root root  314 Sep  7 22:32 CHANGELOG.md
drwxr-xr-x. 2 root root 4096 Jan 18 23:11 clouds
drwxr-xr-x. 4 root root   36 Sep  7 22:32 components
-rw-r--r--. 1 root root   60 Sep  7 22:32 Gemfile
-rw-r--r--. 1 root root 7782 Nov 17 03:01 Gemfile.lock
drwxr-xr-x. 3 root root 4096 Jan 18 19:03 packs
-rw-r--r--. 1 root root  171 Sep  7 22:32 README.md
[root@ip-172-31-52-21 circuit-oneops-1]#
```

In the background, OneOps currently uses the fog API to communicate with various clouds. It certainly helps if the new cloud you are adding to OneOps is supported by the fog API. You can find more details on the fog API and the clouds it supports at `https://github.com/fog`. As you can see right out-of-the-box, fog supports a ton of clouds. It is quite possible to add a cloud that is not supported by the fog API since the backend scripts are currently implemented in Chef. However, to do so, the prudent approach would be to add the support for the chosen cloud to the fog API first and then add the support for that cloud to OneOps. To demonstrate how to add support for a currently unsupported cloud to OneOps, we shall be adding support for the **DigitalOcean** cloud.

Understanding the cloud

Before we start to add a support for any given cloud to OneOps, we must have a good understanding of the cloud itself. As a developer, this involves you having a deep understanding of the functioning of the cloud at a manual level, its terminology, offerings, costs, features, naming convention, any quirks, and its shortcomings. If you are going to operate in a multicloud environment, you should also understand how your cloud will behave and coexist with other clouds. Every cloud vendor also offers an API that is usually called by the fog backend. Although the documentation on fog is extensive, you, as a developer, should be familiar with this backend API for the cloud since at some point, you may need to extend or implement it yourself. So, let's do a quick walkthrough of DigitalOcean and its offerings. Unlike some other cloud providers, DigitalOcean does not provide any free offerings or a free trial. You can sign up for an account by going to `https ://www.digitalocean.com/`. You will need to provide a credit card to sign up, and you will be charged for any VMs that you spin up. Please read the charging policies for your cloud very carefully. For example, DigitalOcean charges for VMs that are switched off because in that state too they consume CPU and disk cycles. The DigitalOcean term for a virtual machine is **droplet**. Once you create an account and fill in the required details, you can log in to your account at `https://cloud.digitalocean.com/login`. Over here, you will see options to manually create droplets from pre-existing images, create droplets from your previous snapshots, create and attach Volumes to your droplets, define networking options, define security for your droplets, and access other settings. Like most other clouds, DigitalOcean also provides access to most droplet, Networking, Volume, and Security function via a set of RESTful APIs. To access the API remotely, you will need to generate a personal access token. You can generate the token at `https://cloud.digitalocean.com/s ettings/api/tokens`. Token, once generated, can be accessed only once. So, be sure to copy and paste it some place secure. You will not have access to this token again. Should you lose it, you must discard this token and generate a new token. Also, be sure to limit access to the token as this token will have full rights to the account although you can certainly restrict write option. However, if you do so, your OneOps will not function well, since it needs write access to spin up droplets. You can access the complete DigitalOcean RESTful API documentation at `https://developers.digitalocean.com/documentation/v2/`. To quickly acquaint yourself with the fog DigitalOcean API, you can check out the examples shown at `https://github.com/fog/fog-digitalocean/blob/master/lib/fog/digitalo cean/examples/getting_started.md`.

So, here are the things that you will need to know to successfully spin up a droplet with DigitalOcean. To begin with, you will need to know your **Personal access tokens**. If you don't already have one, go ahead, and generate one at the URL mentioned earlier. Make sure that you give it Read and Write access. Give it an appropriate name.

Source: https://cloud.digitalocean.com/settings/API/tokens

You will also need to know the droplet distribution name and the image name that you need to spin up. Usually, these two are combined in the same string. You can find all the image names available to you by running the command:

```
curl -X GET --silent "https://API.digitalocean.com/v2/images?per_page=999"
-H "Authorization: Bearer $TOKEN" |jq '.' | grep name
```

In the earlier command, the variable TOKEN is the personal access token you generated from the DigitalOcean website.

 Jq is like 'sed' but for json data. It may not exist by default on your system, and you may need to install it.

This will show you all the available image names that you can spin to bring up a droplet:

```
    "name": "WordPress on 14.04",
    "name": "Dokku 0.6.5 on 14.04",
    "name": "ownCloud 9.0.3 on 14.04",
    "name": "Magento 2.0.7 CE on 14.04",
    "name": "LAMP on 14.04",
    "name": "LEMP on 14.04",
    "name": "NodeJS 6.9.1 on 14.04",
    "name": ".NET Core w/ PowerShell on 16.04",
    "name": "Dokku 0.7.2 on 16.04",
    "name": "MEAN 0.5.0 on 16.04",
    "name": "Docker 1.12.4 on 16.04",
    "name": "Ruby-on-Rails 5.0.1 on 16.04",
    "name": "NodeJS 6.9.4 on 16.04",
    "name": "MongoDB 3.2.11 on 16.04",
    "name": "LEMP on 16.04",
    "name": "WordPress 4.7 on 16.04",
    "name": "LAMP on 16.04",
    "name": "Django 1.8.7 on 16.04",
    "name": "Ghost 0.11.4 on 16.04",
    "name": "Docker 1.12.6 on 16.04",
    "name": "GitLab 8.15.4-ce.1 on 16.04",
    "name": "Redmine on 14.04",
[root@ip-172-31-52-21 circuit-oneops-1]#
```

You can spin up a droplet using the `curl` command via command line. Similarly the `fog` library can also be used in scripts to spin up droplets. To do both you must know the image names. Besides this, you will need to know the endpoint for API, which is `https://develo pers.digitalocean.com/`. You will also need to know the size of the droplet you need to create. The size is generally expressed in MB or GB. For example, 512 MB, 1 GB, and 2 GB are valid sizes. There are some standard sizes available and some high memory sizes available. The high memory sizes are available only if you open a special ticket with support.

You will also need to pass on this size as a string to the fog API to create the droplet.

Choose a size

Standard   High memory

$5/mo	$10/mo	$20/mo	$40/mo	$80/mo	$160/mo
$0.007/hour	$0.015/hour	$0.030/hour	$0.060/hour	$0.119/hour	$0.238/hour
512 MB / 1 CPU	1 GB / 1 CPU	2 GB / 2 CPUs	4 GB / 2 CPUs	8 GB / 4 CPUs	16 GB / 8 CPUs
20 GB SSD disk	30 GB SSD disk	40 GB SSD disk	60 GB SSD disk	80 GB SSD disk	160 GB SSD disk
1000 GB transfer	2 TB transfer	3 TB transfer	4 TB transfer	5 TB transfer	6 TB transfer

$320/mo	$480/mo	$640/mo
$0.476/hour	$0.714/hour	$0.952/hour
32 GB / 12 CPUs	48 GB / 16 CPUs	64 GB / 20 CPUs
320 GB SSD disk	480 GB SSD disk	640 GB SSD disk
7 TB transfer	8 TB transfer	9 TB transfer

Source https://cloud.digitalocean.com/droplets/new

The default attached disk size and the available data transfer size is fixed and depends on the size of the droplet. You will also need to know the data center region in which to spin up the droplet. Currently, DigitalOcean provides three data centers in New York, named **nyc1**, **nyc2**, and **nyc3**, two in San Francisco, named **sf1** and **sf2**, two in Amsterdam called **ams1** and **ams2**, and so on. You can see the full list of available data center list at `https://c loud.digitalocean.com/droplets/new`.

Note that not all images are available at all data centers.

Configuring your cloud

Provided you have all this information to start with, let's start configuring our cloud. As mentioned in the previous chapters, all our configuration will go under our circuit. If you have created any custom circuit, make sure to create these configurations and your scripts under that circuit. Assuming that you are working with the default circuit that resides in the directory `/home/oneops/build/circuit-oneops-1` and links to `/opt/oneops/inductor/circuit/oneops-1`; all your tasks will happen within that directory. As step 1, we will create metadata for the cloud `digitalocean`. You can create it using the knife cloud and knife model commands. However, that tends to create too many files. For this exercise to keep things simple and to understand things better, we will create all files and directories manually. First, under `components/cookbooks`, let's create the directory named `digitalocean`. Now you can either create every file here by hand or else you can copy over a directory belonging to another cloud, and then edit the relevant files. The second approach is preferable as that will save you time and a lot of typing. Go ahead and create a copy of `aliyun` and call it `digitalocean`. Aliyun or Alibaba cloud is the latest cloud to be added to OneOps. Now, let's edit the metadata for the cloud. Open the file `digitalocean/metadata.rb` in your favorite editor. This is a Chef recipe and is written in Ruby DSL. Change the name to **Digitalocean**. Note the capital **D**. Add the attributes key and URL as required. You can put a default value for the URL as `https://developers.dig italocean.com/`. Also, add the attributes `region` and `availability_zones`:

```ruby
  }

attribute 'region',
  :description => "Region",
  :default => "",
  :format => {
    :help => 'Region Name',
    :category => '2.Placement',
    :order => 1
  }

attribute 'availability_zones',
  :description => "Availability Zones",
  :data_type => "array",
  :default => '[]',
  :format => {
    :help => 'Availability Zones - Singles will round robin, Redundant will use
platform id',
    :category => '2.Placement',
    :order => 2
  }
```

Note the attributes, `sizemap` and `imagemap`. The `sizemap` attribute defines sizes as understood by OneOps and maps them to corresponding sizes as understood by the cloud. For example, for an instance (or a droplet as DigitalOcean calls it) of small size, OneOps calls it **XS**. However, DigitalOcean calls it 512 MB. This mapping of **XS** to 512 MB can be defined here. Similarly, OneOps has predefined names for images. These names can be mapped to the image names as understood by DigitalOcean in the `imagemap` attribute. For example, for a Centos 7.0 64 bit installation, OneOps calls the image **centos-7.0**, whereas DigitalOcean calls it **centos-7-0-x64**. As we shall see very soon, both attributes can also be overridden in the cloud definition. For now, you can leave the rest of the attributes alone. Think of the attributes as variables that the rest of the services under the cloud can use to store and retrieve data. As the configuration of your cloud progresses, you can always come back here and add more attributes to store more data (for example, things like billing and IP address). Finally, don't forget to add the cloud name, description, the maintainer name, maintainer e-mail id, and license.

Defining your cloud

Once the metadata is defined under `circuit-oneops-1/components/cookbooks/digitalocean/metadata.rb`, you are ready to define the cloud itself and the services that it offers. You can find all the cloud definitions under the directory `circuit-oneops-1/clouds`. Under this directory, you can create a file named `digitalocean.rb`, which will contain your cloud definition. If you notice, the first three lines will be name, `description` and an `auth`. The `auth` can be a random string of your choice. After this, you will see the familiar `image_map`, which will map OneOps friendly image names to DigitalOcean-friendly image names:

```
name "digitalocean"
description "Digitial Ocean"
auth "dosecretkey"
image_map = '{
"centos-7.2":"centos-7-2-x64",
"centos-7.0":"centos-7-0-x64"
}'
```

After this, you will find a repo map that essentially shows what extra repository and software needs to be installed once a compute node is brought up. A separate repo map can be defined for each image that is defined under a cloud. After the repository maps are defined, we finally define the compute service that will be added to the cloud, which will be deploying the compute service. We have the following code:

```
repo_map = '{
        "centos-7.2":"sudo yum clean all;sudo yum -d0 -e0 -y install rsync yum-u
tils; sudo yum -d0 -e0 -y install epel-release; sudo yum -d0 -e0 -y install gcc-
c++",
        "centos-7.0":"sudo yum clean all;sudo yum -d0 -e0 -y install rsync yum-u
tils; sudo yum -d0 -e0 -y install epel-release; sudo yum -d0 -e0 -y install gcc-
c++"
}'

service "digitalocean-droplet",
    :description => 'Digital Ocean Droplet',
    :cookbook => 'digitalocean',
    :source => [Chef::Config[:register], Chef::Config[:version].split(".").first]
.join('.'),
    :provides => { :service => 'compute' },
    :attributes => {
        :region => "",
        :api_key => "",
        :subnet => "",
        :imagemap => image_map,
        :repo_map => repo_map
}
```

As seen in the earlier image, we are calling the service a `digitalocean-droplet`. The description is also appropriately `Digital Ocean Droplet`. The `cookbook` used will be the `digitalocean` droplet. Just mentioning this is enough for us to drop recipes with a suffix of `_digitalocean` in appropriate directories for OneOps to pick up as we shall see shortly. We shall be providing the compute service. The service shall use the region, `api_key`, `subnet`, `imagemap`, and `repo_map` attributes. Instead of using the `imagemap` and `repo_map` from `metadata.rb`, we have overridden their values in the cloud definition file itself.

This is done for no reason other than to demonstrate that it can be done and some attributes such as `imagemap` and `repo_map` are more convenient to store with the cloud definition. Once this is done, you can now sync your metadata, which is your model definition and your cloud definition with your CMS server by issuing the following commands:

```
knife model sync digitalocean
knife cloud sync digitalocean
```

After this is done, you will need to restart the display server for the changes to be reflected in the GUI:

```
[[root@ip-172-31-52-21 circuit-oneops-1]# knife model sync digitalocean
Processing metadata for digitalocean from /home/oneops/build/circuit-oneops-1/co
mponents/cookbooks/digitalocean/metadata.rb
Updating class base.oneops.1.Digitalocean
Successfuly saved class base.oneops.1.Digitalocean
Updating class mgmt.cloud.service.oneops.1.Digitalocean
Successfuly saved class mgmt.cloud.service.oneops.1.Digitalocean
Updating class cloud.service.oneops.1.Digitalocean
Successfuly saved class cloud.service.oneops.1.Digitalocean
remote_dir:
   <Fog::Storage::Local::Directory
   key="cms"
  >
package_name: mgmt.cloud.service
package_name: cloud.service
doc: /home/oneops/build/circuit-oneops-1/components/cookbooks/digitalocean/doc/D
igitalocean.png remote: oneops.1.Digitalocean/Digitalocean.png
doc: /home/oneops/build/circuit-oneops-1/components/cookbooks/digitalocean/doc/D
igitalocean.png remote: service.oneops.1.Digitalocean/Digitalocean.png
doc: /home/oneops/build/circuit-oneops-1/components/cookbooks/digitalocean/doc/D
igitalocean.png remote: service.oneops.1.Digitalocean/Digitalocean.png
[[root@ip-172-31-52-21 circuit-oneops-1]# knife cloud sync digitalocean
Starting sync for cloud digitalocean
```

Once your model and cloud are synced, you should restart your display server for the changes to be reflected in the GUI. Your cloud should now be visible as a destination to be added under clouds.

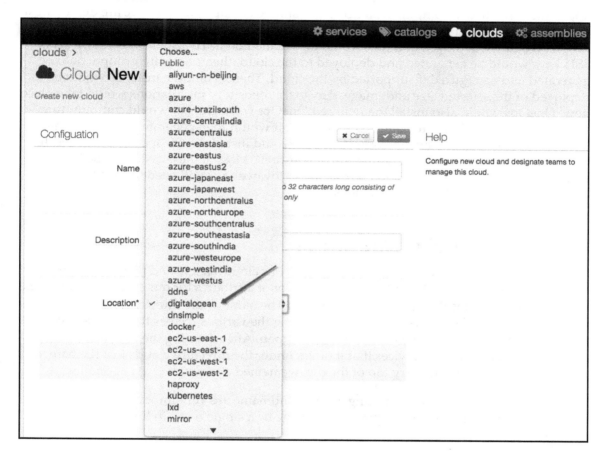

The **digitalocean** droplet is also available to be added as a compute service. However, it's hardly functional as it has no supporting recipes at the backend. If you attempt a deployment, to this cloud and to this service, you will get a ton of errors and the deployment will fail. So, let's remedy the situation by adding a few recipes.

Adding a custom compute instance

Before we can add a compute instance, let's look at the steps needed to deploy an application that uses a compute instance. For a simple example, let's say we are deploying a compute instance and installing java on it. If we were to deploy this on DigitalOcean, a droplet would be deployed and JDK would be installed on it. To achieve this first, a set of SSH keys would be generated and deployed to the cloud, then a security group would be generated and configured if supported by the cloud. Then a compute instance would be deployed of the selected size and image. Any extra repository installations would take place now. OneOps would also install the required OneOps software that would communicate with OneOps and allow it to control the instance. It would then generate FQDN and map the appropriate domain name. Finally, OneOps would install the OS-specific packages. It would then install an appropriate version of JDK on it. Most of these tasks will be handled by the pre-existing cookbooks and their recipes. However, we will need to supply some recipes in some of the existing cookbooks.

How it all works together?

As you noted before, we created a directory with our cloud's name and then created the `metadata.rb` file in it. In that file, we defined a lot of attributes for our cloud. However, the most important part is the name of the directory. The name of the directory, `digitalocean`, will serve as the key to identifying the various recipes that will be picked up from all the places to make various things happen. After defining the metadata, we defined our cloud and the services that it offers under the directory clouds in a file named `digitalocean.rb`. At the very top of the file, we named our cloud `digitalocean`.

 The case and the spacing of the cloud name are very important. It is recommended that your cloud name be a single word in lower case.

This cloud name is then set as the provider name in the workorder for any deployment that will happen. Since OneOps uses Chef (or more accurately Chef-solo) for backend deployments, a little knowledge of Chef comes in handy at this point. When a deployment is fired by the inductor, it makes a list of all cookbooks and their dependencies that need to be run. Chef stores all runnable scripts under what are known as cookbooks, found under components. Cookbooks are groupings of scripts that have a similar purpose. These individual scripts are called recipes. Thus, we have a Cookbook named compute with recipes to add, repair, and delete it. Coming back to the original point, when an inductor fires a deployment, Chef creates a dependency list of all the cookbooks and the recipes under it. It will also read all the metadata and the configuration that it finds. It then creates a configuration object named node, which is a Ruby hash. Inside of node, you can find all the configuration parameters that are defined for the deployment, configuration about the cloud and lots of other information. The cloud name is also set in the node as follows:

```
node[:workorder][:cloud][:ciName]
```

When a deployment goes through various stages, such as SSH key generation, compute, OS, and so on, it calls and executes the cookbooks for the respective steps. Specifically, it executes a recipe relevant to that deployment. For example, if the deployment is adding a new instance, then it will execute the add.rb recipe under the keypair component. It will then execute the add.rb recipe under the compute instance. However, many of the recipes have a line as follows:

```
include_recipe "keypair::add_keypair_"+node[:provider_class]
```

This line was taken from add.rb in the keypair directory under components, which is responsible for generating and adding ssh keys. What it means is if a file named add_keypair_digitalocean.rb exists in that directory include it as a recipe. A variation of this line exists in all add, repair, and delete recipes in most components. This makes it easy to create custom and new recipes for our new cloud without having to change existing recipes. We will take advantage of this feature to create and add new recipes to existing components.

Prerequisites

Before you can start adding recipes, you will need to make two changes to the OneOps admin gem and deploy it again. Assuming that you downloaded the OneOps admin gem, as instructed in Chapter 7, *Working with Functional Components*, locate the file `set_providers.rb` under `lib/shared/cookbooks/shared/recipes`. In this file, you will find a case statement for `provider_class` that sets the provider for various clouds. Add the code given later anywhere before the case statement ends in order to set the provider as `digitalocean` for the fog API when dealing with the `digitalocean` cloud:

```
when /digitalocean/
require 'fog/digitalocean'
provider = Fog::Compute.new({
:provider => 'digitalocean',
:digitalocean_token => cloud[:key]
})
```

Now find the file `oneops-admin.gemspec` and add the following line toward the end of the file:

```
s.add_dependency "fog-digitalocean", '= 0.2.0'
```

The case statement sets the provider as DigitalOcean and creates a compatible object for Fog whenever the cloud type is DigitalOcean. The earlier-mentioned line adds the `fog-digitalocean` gem to the OneOps admin gem as a dependency so that all of our deployments will work well. Once this is done, we will need to compile and deploy the OneOps admin gem again.

 If you have built OneOps since the last time, you built and deployed OneOps Admin, be sure to copy the latest inductor jar to the target directory. You can usually find the inductor jar in `/home/oneops/dist/oneops/dist`.

Build and deploy OneOps admin using the commands here:

```
gem build oneops-admin.gemspec
gem install oneops-admin
```

Generating SSH keys

As the first step to deployments, OneOps generates SSH keys for the VM--a public key and a private key. Some clouds give you the option of storing your own SSH keys in the cloud, which you can then use to spin up instances and associate with certain accounts on the instance. This makes it convenient and secure for you to log in to the server if you possess the private key. In instances where a cloud does not provide you with the facility to store the SSH key on the cloud side, you must copy the SSH key over to the instance after it is live and associate it with an account, usually root, manually. Fortunately, not only does DigitalOcean provide you with option to upload your own SSH keys but also provides an API to manipulate them. This way, you can generate and upload your SSH keys before spinning up a droplet and then associate it with an account, just in the order that OneOps does. Now, let's create a file named `add_keypair_digitalocean.rb` under `components/cookbooks/keypair/recipes`. As mentioned earlier, this file will be called by `add.rb` when the SSH keypairs are generated:

```ruby
require 'fog/digitalocean'


cloud_name = node[:workorder][:cloud][:ciName]
attributes = node[:workorder][:services][:compute][cloud_name][:ciAttributes]
Chef::Log.debug("Public key: " + node.keypair.public)
conn = Fog::Compute.new({
   :provider => 'DigitalOcean',
   :digitalocean_token => attributes[:key]
})
key = conn.ssh_keys.get(node.kp_name)
if key == nil
   key = conn.ssh_keys.create(
       :name => node.kp_name,
       :ssh_pub_key => node.keypair.public,
       :public_key => node.keypair.public
   )
   Chef::Log.info("import keypair: " + key.inspect)
else
   Chef::Log.info("existing keypair: #{key.inspect}")
end

"add_keypair_digitalocean.rb" 22L, 626C
```

Note that we added the requisite library `fog/digitalocean` at the top. Also not the syntax to create keys `ssh_keys.create` is specific to DigitalOcean. To open an authenticated connection to DigitalOcean, all we need is the token that was defined in the attributes. We can obtain the token by first obtaining the attributes from the node object and the specifically looking up the key.

In hindsight, token was probably a better choice of name rather than key. Key could be confused with the SSH key. In such cases, you can always go back to `metadata.rb` and change the attribute. If you do that, don't forget to `run knife sync <model | cloud> <yourcloudname>` to sync your cloud with CMS. For now, we will leave the name alone as this is the only place it is used.

If the recipe finds an existing keypair, it then imports the keys, and if the recipe does not, it generates and uploads the keys. After this step of the deployment runs, if you check the DigtalOcean side, you will find an SSH key has been uploaded successfully.

SSH keys		Add SSH Key
Name	**Fingerprint**	
oneops_key.140653.devruby.140687	9f:73:18:4f:18:5d:96:c4:44:0f:e7:f0:27:95:14:51	More ∨
oneops_key.137799.Dev.137834	21:2d:dd:6b:d3:fe:4a:95:e2:42:49:85:4f:f6:3d:92	More ∨

Internally, DigitalOcean can identify the key via its name, ID, or its fingerprint. We will be using its name to identify it as that's what OneOps stores and associates with the assembly. One last thing we need to do is add a recipe to delete the keypair for `digitalocean` named `del_keypair_digitalocean.rb`. The recipe looks very like `add recipe`, except, it deletes the keypair from OneOps and DigitalOcean when an assembly is deleted. We have the following code:

```
#
# supports openstack keypair::delete
#
cloud_name = node[:workorder][:cloud][:ciName]
token = node[:workorder][:services][:compute][cloud_name][:ciAttributes]

conn = Fog::Compute.new({
  :provider => 'DigitalOcean',
  :digitalocean_token => token[:key]
})
node.set["kp_name"] = node.kp_name.gsub(".","-")

# delete if exists
if !conn.ssh_keys.get(node.kp_name).nil?

  conn.ssh_key.destroy(node.kp_name)
  Chef::Log.info("deleted keypair: #{node.kp_name}")

else
  Chef::Log.info("already deleted keypair: #{node.kp_name}")
end
~
"del_keypair_digitalocean.rb" 21L, 537C
```

Adding the compute recipe

After the key pairs are added, technically, the next step is the generation and adding of security groups. However, DigitalOcean does not really support the concept of security groups, so this step can be skipped for now. We can now directly go to the compute cookbook. Inside the directory `components/cookbooks/compute/recipe`, create a file named `add_node_digitalocean.rb`. It helps if you read some existing recipes and see how they control their clouds and acquaint yourself with the `fog-digitalocean` (or the API for your cloud) to see how they control their cloud. It also helps if you copy over an existing recipe and start editing it instead of writing one from scratch. You can start by copying over the *alyiyun* or *openstack* recipe. However, be sure to change the attributes, `providers` and `syntax`, to your cloud. Now, let's see if we can make sense of the recipe piece by piece. At the very top of the recipe, we parse various attributes for the cloud and store them in local variables for later use. Attributes, such as cloud name, image map, connection, and size map, that we defined earlier are all extracted from metadata or other sources and set here:

```
cloud_name = node[:workorder][:cloud][:ciName]
token = node[:workorder][:services][:compute][cloud_name][:ciAttributes]
conn = Fog::Compute.new({
```

```
:provider => 'DigitalOcean',
:digitalocean_token => token[:key]
})
rfcCi = node[:workorder][:rfcCi]
Chef::Log.debug("rfcCi attrs:"+rfcCi[:ciAttributes].inspect.gsub("n"," "))
nsPathParts = rfcCi[:nsPath].split("/")
security_domain = nsPathParts[3]+'.'+nsPathParts[2]+'.'+nsPathParts[1]
Chef::Log.debug("security domain: "+ security_domain)
# size / flavor
sizemap = JSON.parse( token[:sizemap] )
size_id = sizemap[rfcCi[:ciAttributes][:size]]
Chef::Log.info("flavor: #{size_id}")
```

Also, note that we are making liberal use of Chef log messages in info and debug mode to make it easy to debug our installation. The info and debug messages show up in different colors to aid easy debugging during installation. We then check whether the server was supposed to be replaced or, if the server was already deployed and was active or in stopped state, we simply update the server name:

```
if ! rfcCi["ciAttributes"]["instance_id"].nil? &&
! rfcCi["ciAttributes"]["instance_id"].empty? &&
! rfcCi["rfcAction"] == "replace"
server = conn.servers.get(rfcCi["ciAttributes"]["instance_id"])
else
#server = conn.servers.find { |i| i.name == node.server_name }
conn.servers.all.each do |s|
Chef::Log.info("server's name: #{s.inspect}")
Chef::Log.info("Server name: " + s.name)
Chef::Log.info("Server status: " + s.status)
if s.name == node.server_name && (s.status == "active" || s.status ==
"stopped")
server = s
break
end
end
end
```

If none of those conditions are met, we will create a new droplet. However, before we can create the droplet, we need to find the ID of the SSH key that was created and uploaded to DigitalOcean as part of the deployment. We simply loop through all the keys available on DigitalOcean under our account and if the key name matches the key name of our current assembly, we store the corresponding ID in a variable:

```
conn.ssh_keys.each do | key |
if key.name == node.kp_name
ssh_key_id = key.id.to_s
end
end
```

Once that is done, we are ready to create a droplet with the required details:

```
server = conn.servers.create(
:image => node[:image_id],
:size => size_id,
:region => token[:region],
:name => node.server_name,
:ssh_keys => [ssh_key_id]
)
done = true
```

We now wait for the server to come up. Do keeps the status of the droplet as new for 60 to 90 seconds while it initializes it. This means it is bringing up all the services, installing miscellaneous software and so on. After which it changes the status to active. OneOps does not recognize the droplet as up till the status changes to active. We will try for max 30 attempts. In addition we will sleep for 30 seconds between attempts. The server should be active after two or three attempts:

```
ok=false
attempt=0
max_attempts=30
while !ok && attempt<max_attempts
if (server.ready?)
public_ip = server.public_ip_address
ok = true
else
Chef::Log.info("current status " + server.status)
Chef::Log.info("waiting for the server in active state")
attempt += 1
sleep 30
end
end
```

Once the server is active, we find its public IP address. The recipe can, at this point, hand over control to the main `add.rb`, which then continues with the installation of required software, and so on.

The cloud is now ready to use. It can be added as any other cloud to OneOps and will show up in the cloud's list.

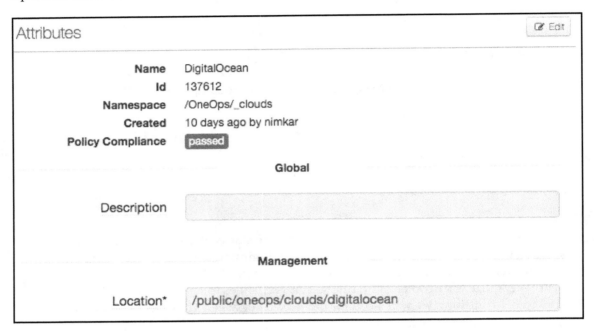

Your compute service will also show up and will be available for use. You can add it to your cloud or other clouds as you like.

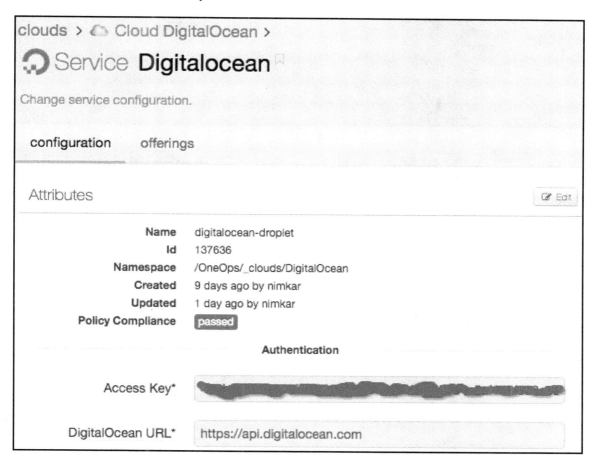

Note the **DigitalOcean** logo next to the compute service. If your cloud has a logo that you can download and would like to show up next to your cloud and compute service, simply create a doc directory under your cloud directory where you created your `metadata.rb`. In our case, I created the doc directory under `components/cookbooks/digitalocean` and placed a file there called `Digitalocean.png`. I then ran the command here:

```
knife model sync digitalocean
```

Once done, the logo showed up in OneOps. You are now ready to do a test deployment to test out the new cloud.

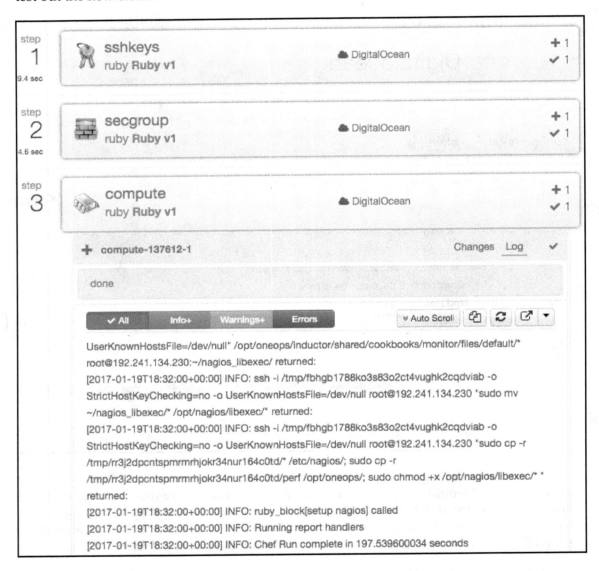

Summary

In this chapter, we saw how to add a custom cloud to OneOps. Although we saw how to add a single service, a compute service, the steps to add any service to OneOps is pretty much the same, provided you understand the underlying structuring and functioning of OneOps and how it interacts with the cloud. This was demonstrated when we added SSH keys to DigitalOcean before we added the droplet and then we queried the same SSH keys from the droplet recipe before the droplet was created. Although we saw the code piece by piece to understand it better, the code in its entirety is available for download from GitHub. In the next chapter, we will see how to extend the OneOps functionality by taking advantage of OneOps's RESTful API. We will control various aspects of OneOps through scripts without touching the GUI using Ruby as our choice of scripting language.

11
Integrating with OneOps Using API

In the previous chapter, we saw how to add a brand new cloud to OneOps. This concluded what started a few chapters ago when we added new components and created packs. OneOps is very robust and extensible, and it allows you to create components and packs with ease. However, if you have existing systems and processes in place, you can easily integrate OneOps in your workflow using the OneOps REST API interface. In this chapter, we shall take a brief overview of the REST API provided by OneOps along with a few practical examples of how we can achieve things from outside OneOps.

Prerequisites

Assuming that you want to automate and integrate your systems with OneOps using the REST interface, you should have a functional knowledge of what REST is and how a typical REST API functions. REST stands for REpresentational State Transfer. It is a web standards-based architecture where everything is represented as a resource, and it can be accessed using standard HTTP methods, such as GET, PUT, POST, and DELETE. Data is usually passed back and forth between the client and server in text, XML, or JSON. JSON is the preferred format lately.

 REST is a stateless protocol. This means that, between requests, no session is maintained. Hence, each request is self-contained and must contain all the state information required to fulfill that request.

Thus, using the REST architecture OneOps provides a set of RESTful web services that can be accessed using unique **Uniform Resource Identifiers (URIs)**.

 Most of requests made to a RESTful resource are idempotent. This means that multiple requests with the same parameters made against the same resource will always yield the same result, although there are exceptions to this rule.

Before you can start using the REST API, you must set up yourself to authenticate with OneOps using REST. To do so, log in to your OneOps instance, then click on your login name in the lower left-hand corner to go to your profile page. Click on the **authentication** tab. On this tab, you can change your password as well as access to your **API Token**. You can also regenerate your API token to a different one if you want.

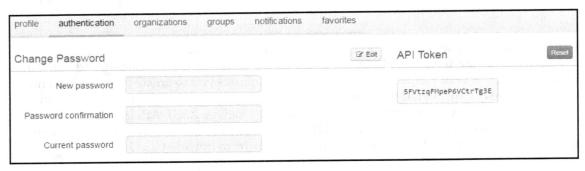

The API token serves as a unique alias for your username and provides a measure of security since it is passed as a clear text using basic authentication. In any tool or language that you use to access the REST API, you should use this token wherever you would use the username and leave the password empty. You can even use a command line to access the REST resources:

```
server="<your OneOps Server URL>"
resource="/account/organizations"
command="${server}${resource}"
curl -i -u <your OneOps Token>: -H "Content-Type:application/json" -H
"Accept:application/json" -X GET -v ${command}
```

This command should give you all the organizations that your account has access to.

```
[centos@ip-172-31-52-21 ~]$ curl -i -u "5FVtzqFMpeP6VCtrTg3E": -H "Content-Type:applic
ation/json" -H "Accept:application/json" -X GET -v ${command} 2>/dev/null
HTTP/1.1 200 OK
X-Frame-Options: SAMEORIGIN
X-Xss-Protection: 1; mode=block
X-Content-Type-Options: nosniff
Cache-Control: no-cache, no-store, max-age=0, must-revalidate
Pragma: no-cache
Expires: Thu, 01 Jan 1970 00:00:00 GMT
Access-Control-Allow-Origin: *
Access-Control-Allow-Methods: POST, GET, PUT, DELETE, OPTIONS
Access-Control-Allow-Headers: Origin, X-Requested-With, Token, Authorization, Content-
Type, Accept
Access-Control-Max-Age: 86400
Content-Type: application/json; charset=utf-8
X-Request-Id: e5a703bb-6cbd-4d12-adde-b52ce95fb2b4
X-Runtime: 0.009669
Server: WEBrick/1.3.1 (Ruby/2.0.0/2014-11-13)
Date: Fri, 10 Mar 2017 02:36:09 GMT
Content-Length: 430
Connection: Keep-Alive

[{"id":1,"name":"OneOps","created_at":"2016-09-07T22:43:13.969Z","updated_at":"2016-09
-29T21:10:58.077Z","cms_id":108071,"assemblies":true,"catalogs":true,"services":true,"
announcement":"","full_name":"OneOps"},{"id":2,"name":"MyOrg","created_at":"2016-10-06
T17:15:28.553Z","updated_at":"2016-10-06T17:15:44.903Z","cms_id":118684,"assemblies":t
rue,"catalogs":true,"services":false,"announcement":"","full_name":"My Organization"}]
[centos@ip-172-31-52-21 ~]$
```

As you can see, since we requested output in JSON by specifying the `Content-Type` as application/JSON, the output was supplied in JSON. The same effect can also be achieved by adding "`.json`" at the end of any resource. So, if in the earlier example we had set the resource to "`/accounts/organization.json`", we would have gotten the same result. Also, when we provided the user ID with the option -u, we provided it as-- "`<your OneOps token>:`". Note that there is a colon "`:`" after the token and then nothing after the colon. As mentioned before, the token serves as a replacement for the username. If we use the token, and we must use it if we want to use the REST API, then we need to provide only the token and no password. Since the -u option takes the username and password separated by a colon, we just type the token and a colon and leave the rest blank.

Connecting to the REST API using Ruby

The beauty of RESTful services and using JSON or XML to communicate over the web is that you can use any modern language (and many not-so-modern languages) to quickly and efficiently talk to OneOps. Since, so far, all our coding has been in Ruby, or to be specific in Chef, we will be using Ruby as an example language for this chapter. However, since the resources are idempotent, the language itself rarely matters. Before we can start using Ruby though, let's make sure that the appropriate dependencies are satisfied. Since we will be building our own custom REST client, we will be using a Ruby gem named `rest-client`. You can install it using the command:

```
gem install rest-client
```

Also, make sure that `gem json` is installed. You can install it by running the following command:

```
gem install json
```

For `rest-client`, you should have MRI Ruby 2.0 or higher installed. If you are trying this from a OneOps instance, then Ruby 2.0 or higher should already be installed.

```
[[root@ip-172-31-52-21 ~]# gem install rest-client
Successfully installed rest-client-2.0.1
1 gem installed
[[root@ip-172-31-52-21 ~]# gem install json
Building native extensions.  This could take a while...
Successfully installed json-2.0.3
1 gem installed
[[root@ip-172-31-52-21 ~]# ruby -v
ruby 2.0.0p598 (2014-11-13) [x86_64-linux]
[root@ip-172-31-52-21 ~]#
```

Once both gems are installed, you are now ready to write your scripts. The added advantage of using `rest-client` is that it comes with a command-line console that easily allows you to test your resources. To launch the console, run the following command:

```
restclient<url for your OneOps instance> "<OneOps token>" ""
```

This will launch the `rest-client` console connected to your OneOps instance. You can then try out various resources before writing your scripts.

 Note the empty quotes at the end of the afore-mentioned command. They are for the password, which is empty because we are supplying a token.

```
[root@ip-172-31-52-21 ~]# restclient http://ec2-54-91-111-194.compute-1.amazonaws.com:
3000 "5FVtzqFMpeP6VCtrTg3E" ""
irb(main):001:0> require "json"
=> true
irb(main):002:0> response = JSON.parse(get "/account/organizations")
=> [{"id"=>1, "name"=>"OneOps", "created_at"=>"2016-09-07T22:43:13.969Z", "updated_at"
=>"2016-09-29T21:10:58.077Z", "cms_id"=>108071, "assemblies"=>true, "catalogs"=>true,
"services"=>true, "announcement"=>"", "full_name"=>"OneOps"}, {"id"=>2, "name"=>"MyOrg
", "created_at"=>"2016-10-06T17:15:28.553Z", "updated_at"=>"2016-10-06T17:15:44.903Z",
 "cms_id"=>118684, "assemblies"=>true, "catalogs"=>true, "services"=>false, "announcem
ent"=>"", "full_name"=>"My Organization"}]
irb(main):003:0> response[1]["name"]
=> "MyOrg"
irb(main):004:0> 
```

As you can see in the earlier screenshot, we launched the REST console against a test OneOps instance. We then loaded the `json gem`. We then requested the organizations that we have access to, just like we did from the command line. Because the data required is in JSON format, we parsed the JSON data into a Ruby data structure. A quick examination shows us that we have two organizations. By accessing the data structure, we can then print the name of the second organization. Now, let's see whether, by using the same method, we can figure out what the first cloud is under our very first organization. Again, let's start by connecting to the `rest-client` by issuing the `restclient` command, if you are not connected already. We will issue the same command as before, only this time we will capture the result in a variable. We will then use the variable to query what clouds are configured under that organization. Overall the list of commands looks as follows:

```
require 'json'
response = JSON.parse(get "/account/organizations")
orgName = response[0]["name"]
JSON.parse(get "/#{orgName}/clouds.json")[0]["ciName"]
```

After we run these commands we can see from the output that the cloud that shows up is in fact the DigitalOcean cloud that we created.

```
[root@ip-172-31-52-21 ~]# restclient http://ec2-54-91-111-194.compute-1.amazonaws.com:
3000 "5FVtzqFMpeP6VCtrTg3E" ""
irb(main):001:0> require 'json'
=> true
irb(main):002:0> response = JSON.parse(get "/account/organizations")
=> [{"id"=>1, "name"=>"OneOps", "created_at"=>"2016-09-07T22:43:13.969Z", "updated_at"
=>"2016-09-29T21:10:58.077Z", "cms_id"=>108071, "assemblies"=>true, "catalogs"=>true,
"services"=>true, "announcement"=>"", "full_name"=>"OneOps"}, {"id"=>2, "name"=>"MyOrg
", "created_at"=>"2016-10-06T17:15:28.553Z", "updated_at"=>"2016-10-06T17:15:44.903Z",
 "cms_id"=>118684, "assemblies"=>true, "catalogs"=>true, "services"=>false, "announcem
ent"=>"", "full_name"=>"My Organization"}]
irb(main):003:0> orgName = response[0]["name"]
=> "OneOps"
irb(main):004:0> JSON.parse(get "/#{orgName}/clouds.json")[0]["ciName"]
=> "DOCloud"
irb(main):005:0>
```

This of course assumes that you know where all your OneOps goodies are kept and how to refer to them. If you do not know or if your OneOps data gets too large, then there are a couple of things you can do to find various things in OneOps. The easiest thing to do is to use the excellent search feature provided by OneOps. You can access this by clicking on **Search** on the left-hand side menu. This will bring up the global search. You can also search within an assembly by clicking on a particular assembly and then on any environment under it. You should see a search (magnifying glass) icon on the top, which will localize the search just to that assembly.

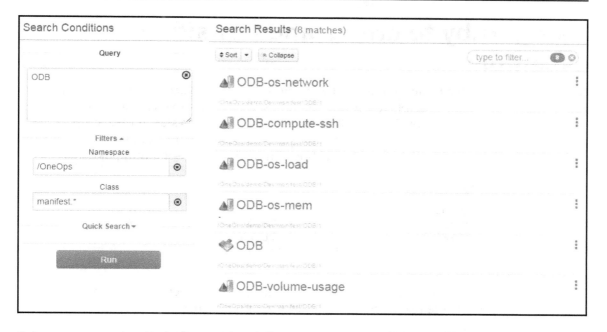

As you can see, you can enter search criteria in the query. The namespace is already filtered for you by the organization in which you are currently searching. You can filter it further if you want for some fine-grained searching. If you want to find an object in a particular phase you can do that by specifying the class. Remember, `catalog.*` is for design phase objects, `manifest.*` is for transition phase objects, and `bom.*` is for operation phase objects. This field also conveniently provides autocomplete to help you select the appropriate class. If you are unsure of the exact class but know the phase, then simply add a `".*"` after the appropriate phase to see everything that matches. By default, search shows items that are cached in the OneOps ElasticSearch instance. You can also load the advance search option, which will directly query the CMS database and give you more filtering choices by appending `"?source=cms"` at the end of search URL. This loads advanced search options. It will now allow you to filter the scope by account, cloud services, design, transition, or operation. You can also filter by any class or attribute name to better locate your objects.

Using Ruby to create and transition assembly

Now that we know the basics of the REST API and know how to access it via the command line, we can start writing scripts to do various things. Our goal is to create an assembly, add some platforms to it, and transition it, all through a script. So, let's start with a simple script and see if we can build on top of it. We start by porting what we did from the command line to a Ruby script, accessing our organization. Our script looks something like this:

```ruby
require 'rest-client'
require 'json'
token = 'CMS8qQDddG1AZxazkTz5'
server = 'http://localhost:9090'
client = RestClient::Resource.new(server,token,'')
result = client['/account/organizations'].get
puts result
```

If you save the script and run it, you can see the output also as given later. Of course, you will have to substitute the token and server with your own values.

```
bash-3.2$ ruby assembley.rb
[{"id":1,"name":"OneOps","created_at":"2017-03-12T12:42:22.537Z","updated_at":"2
017-03-12T12:43:01.204Z","cms_id":146449,"assemblies":true,"catalogs":true,"serv
ices":true,"announcement":"","full_name":"OneOps"}]
bash-3.2$
```

As you can see, the output is as expected. Now let's modify the code a little and see if we can create an assembly:

```ruby
require 'rest-client'
require 'json'
token = 'CMS8qQDddG1AZxazkTz5'
server = 'http://localhost:9090'
assembly = "test"

payload = {
  :cms_ci => {
        :ciName => assembly,
        :comments => "assembley to test the REST API",
        :ciAttributes => {
              :owner => "nilesh@releasemanagement.org",
              :description => "this assembly was created via REST API"
        }
    }
```

```
    }
client = RestClient::Resource.new(server,token,'')

result = client["/OneOps/assemblies.json"].post(payload.to_json,
{content_type: :json, accept: :json})
puts "Assembly created => #{result}"
```

We only made slight additions and modifications to the code. The first two lines are self-explanatory. We need the `rest-client` and `json` module included in the script. We then create variables for token, server, and assembly names that need creating. We then create a payload that we will be sending to the server. The payload is created as a Ruby hash of hash. However, when we send it to the server, we will be converting it to JSON. We then create a connection to the client and call the post method on `"/OneOps/assemblies"`. We pass the payload that we created as a parameter to the post method. We also pass a few parameters telling the server that the parameters we are passing are in the JSON format and the output we are expecting is also in the JSON format. The payload that we constructed should be in a specified format. Since we are creating an assembly, OneOps expects certain parameters to be passed to it. For example, for the creation of an assembly, OneOps expects a hash by the name `"cms_ci"` to be passed to it. The minimum values that it must have are `ciName` and `ciAttributes`. The `ciAttributes` is a hash, and it must also contain a value for the owner, which is usually an e-mail ID. If these values are not contained in the payload, the request will fail. If you provide everything properly, you can now save your file as `assembly.rb` and run it from the command line. It should create the assembly and show its details as the result.

```
bash-3.2$ ruby assembley.rb
{"ciId":146473,"ciName":"test","ciClassName":"account.Assembly","impl":"oo::chef
-11.4.0","nsPath":"/OneOps","ciGoid":"146451-1005-146473","comments":"assembley
to test the REST API","ciState":"default","lastAppliedRfcId":0,"createdBy":"nimk
ar","updatedBy":null,"created":1489438234295,"updated":1489438234295,"nsId":1464
51,"ciAttributes":{"owner":"nilesh@releasemanagement.org","description":"this as
sembly was created via REST API","tags":"{}"},"attrProps":{}}
bash-3.2$
```

You can also log in to the GUI and confirm that your assembly has been created properly with all the parameters that you supplied.

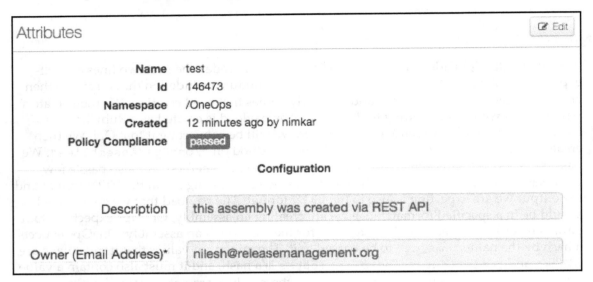

But, as we know, an assembly is an empty box till we add some packs to it. So, now let's modify our script to add a platform to it as soon as it is created. Since we need the assembly's name to add the packs, we already defined it in a variable. We will simply add the part adding a pack to our assembly to the end of the script. If you are unsure what packs are accessible to you, you can always query them by issuing a get request to `"/OneOps/catalog/packs.json"` assuming that your organization name is OneOps. Our modified script looks like this:

```
require 'rest-client'
require 'json'
token = 'CMS8qQDddG1AZxazkTz5'
server = 'http://localhost:9090'
assembly = "test"
platform = "java"
payload = {
  :cms_ci => {
        :ciName => assembly,
        :comments => "assembley to test the REST API",
        :ciAttributes => {
            :owner => "nilesh@releasemanagement.org",
            :description => "this assembly was created via REST API"
        }
    }
}
```

```
client = RestClient::Resource.new(server,token,'')
result = client["/OneOps/assemblies.json"].post(payload.to_json,
{content_type: :json, accept: :json})

puts "Assembley created => #{result}"

payload = {
:cms_dj_ci => {
:comments => "adding java pack",
    :ciName => platform,
    :ciAttributes => {
                :source => "oneops",
                :description => "adding oneops pack to platform",
                :major_version => "1",
                :pack => platform,
                :version => "1"
        }
    }
}
result = client["/OneOps/assemblies/#{assembly}/design/platforms.json"].
post(payload.to_json,{content_type: :json, accept: :json})
puts "Platform #{platform} added => #{result}"
payload = {
  :comment => "Initial comment"
}
result =
client["/OneOps/assemblies/#{assembly}/design/platforms/#{platform}/commit.
json"].post(payload.to_json),{content_type: :json, accept: :json}

puts "Platform #{platform} commited #{result}"
```

As you can see, we simply continued building on the script that we initially created. Also, since REST is a session-less API, you will note two things about the script. First, we are maintaining the same client throughout the script that we initially created; second, our script is doing the job of maintaining the information about session state, in this case the assembly it is working on and the pack it is adding and so on. In advanced scripts, this information can get quite complex, but it can also be queried on-the-fly from OneOps. In our script, as in the previous one, we first created the assembly by creating the payload. In our variables, we have added a new one for the platform, JAVA. In order to add a pack to our assembly, we create a payload by reusing the same variable payload. In this case, OneOps expects this hash--"cms_dj_ci". Again, the values for name and ciAttributes are required. Under ciAttributes, values for source, major_version, pack, and version are required. Once the payload is defined, we call post on the assembly that we created under a design/platform. The complete resource is "/<Your Organization>/assemblies/<Your assembley>/design/platforms.json".

However, once we call `post`, we note that the pack is added but is not committed. So, as a last step, we add a step to commit the pack that we just added. For this, we again create a simple payload with a single variable in it called comment with a very simple comment. We then call `post` on the platform that we just created. The complete resource is "/<Your Organization>/assemblies/<Your assembley>/design/platforms/<platform name>/commit.json". Now if you run the script, it should create the assembly, add the pack to the platform, and then commit it.

```
Assembley created => {"ciId":146653,"ciName":"test","ciClassName":"account.Assem
bley","impl":"oo::chef-11.4.0","nsPath":"/OneOps","ciGoid":"146451-1005-146653","
comments":"assembley to test the REST API","ciState":"default","lastAppliedRfcId
":0,"createdBy":"nimkar","updatedBy":null,"created":1489463826697,"updated":1489
463826697,"nsId":146451,"ciAttributes":{"owner":"nilesh@releasemanagement.org","
description":"this assembly was created via REST API","tags":"{}"},"attrProps":{
}}
Platform java added => {"rfcId":1340,"releaseId":1339,"ciId":146660,"nsPath":"/O
neOps/test","ciClassName":"catalog.Platform","impl":"oo::chef-11.4.0","ciName":"
java","ciGoid":"146657-1102-146660","ciState":null,"rfcAction":"add","releaseTyp
e":null,"createdBy":"nimkar","updatedBy":null,"rfcCreatedBy":"nimkar","rfcUpdate
dBy":null,"execOrder":0,"lastAppliedRfcId":null,"comments":"adding java pack","i
sActiveInRelease":true,"rfcCreated":1489463826831,"rfcUpdated":1489463826831,"cr
eated":1489463826831,"updated":1489463826831,"ciAttributes":{"major_version":"1"
,"description":"adding oneops pack to platform","pack_digest":"cdeb7b3bc668de4e9
032a6d314792a84","source":"oneops","pack":"java","version":"1"},"ciBaseAttribute
s":{},"ciAttrProps":{}}
Platform java commited ["{\"rfcId\":1340,\"releaseId\":1339,\"ciId\":146660,\"ns
Path\":\"/OneOps/test\",\"ciClassName\":\"catalog.Platform\",\"impl\":\"oo::chef
-11.4.0\",\"ciName\":\"java\",\"ciGoid\":\"146657-1102-146660\",\"ciState\":null
,\"rfcAction\":\"add\",\"releaseType\":null,\"createdBy\":\"nimkar\",\"updatedBy
\":null,\"rfcCreatedBy\":\"nimkar\",\"rfcUpdatedBy\":null,\"execOrder\":0,\"last
AppliedRfcId\":null,\"comments\":\"adding java pack\",\"isActiveInRelease\":true
,\"rfcCreated\":1489463826831,\"rfcUpdated\":1489463826831,\"created\":148946382
```

You can also log in to the GUI and verify that the assembly has been created as per the instruction in the script.

Now that the assembly has been created successfully, we can also transition it to an environment via our script. Again, we can make simple changes to the script to transition it to environments that we have. For brevity's sake, I already created a cloud named AWS and then created an environment named dev that will deploy to AWS. However, the same environment can be created be using the REST API too. You can do so by calling PUT on the resource "<Your Organization>/assemblies/<Your assembly>/transition/<Your Environment>/platforms/<Your Platform>/cloud_configuration. You will have to attach the payload, as follows:

```
{
  "cloud_id" : "<cloud ci-id>",
  "attributes" : {
      "adminstatus" : "active or inactive or offline"
      "priority" : "1 or 2"
      "pct_scale" : "...",
      "dpmt_order" : "..."
  }
}
```

Once you have added an environment to your assembly, you are ready to commit and deploy it. We can again modify our previous script to commit our changes to deployment and then initiate the deployment. This assumes that you have already created an environment named `dev` as mentioned earlier. We can again quickly modify our script to commit our deployment and then initiate the actual deployment:

```
require 'rest-client'
require 'json'
token = 'CMS8qQDddG1AZxazkTz5'
server = 'http://localhost:9090'
assembly = "test"
platform = "java"
environment = "dev"
payload = {
  :cms_ci => {
          :ciName => assembly,
          :comments => "assembley to test the REST API",
          :ciAttributes => {
                  :owner => "nilesh@releasemanagement.org",
                  :description => "this assembly was created via REST API"
          }
      }
}
client = RestClient::Resource.new(server,token,'')
result = client["/OneOps/assemblies.json"].post(payload.to_json,
{content_type: :json, accept: :json})
puts "Assembley created => #{result}"
payload = {
  :cms_dj_ci => {
          :comments => "adding java pack",
          :ciName => platform,
          :ciAttributes => {
                  :source => "oneops",
                  :description => "adding oneops pack to platform",
                  :major_version => "1",
                  :pack => platform,
                  :version => "1"
          }
      }
}
result = client["/OneOps/assemblies/#{assembly}/design/platforms.json"]
.post(payload.to_json,{content_type: :json, accept: :json})
puts "Platform #{platform} added => #{result}"
payload = {
  :comment => "Initial comment"
}
result =
```

```
client["/OneOps/assemblies/#{assembly}/design/platforms/#{platform}/commit.
json"].post(payload.to_json),
{content_type: :json, accept: :json}
puts "Platform #{platform} commited #{result}"
payload = {
  :comment => "Initial Deployment"
}
result =
client["/OneOps/assemblies/#{assembly}/transition/environments/#{dev}/commi
t.js"].post(payload.to_json),{content_type: :json, accept: :json}
puts "Deployment Commited => #{result}"
result = JSON.parse(get
"/OneOps/assemblies/#{assembly}/transition/environments/#{environment}/rele
ases/bom")
releaseId = result["releaseId"]
nsPath = result["nsPath"]
payload = {
  :cms_deployment => {
          :releaseId => "#{releaseId}",
          :nsPath => "#{nsPath}"
      }
}
result =
client["/OneOps/assemblies/#{assembly}/transition/environments/#{environmen
t}/deployment.json"].post(payload.to_json),{content_type: :json, accept:
:json}
puts "Deployment Initiated => #{result}"
```

As you can see, we have made a few changes to the script. We have added a new variable named environment, which refers to our environment named dev. We then commit out deployment before initialing it. For this we must create a payload with a variable named commit. After that we have to initiate the deployment; however, before we do that, we have to query the nsPath and the releaseId of the commit that we just did. We can do so by calling get on the resource "/<Your Organization>/assemblies/<Your assembly>/transiton/environments/<Your Environment>/releases/bom" and converting the output to JSON.

We then create a payload with the requisite `releaseId` and `nsPath` and initiate the release. Once the release has been initiated, you can confirm the successful release from the GUI.

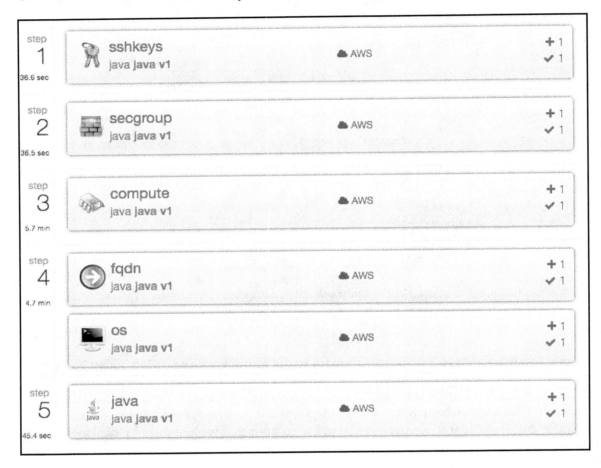

Otherwise, you can also loop over the result returned by the script to see the state of the deployment.

Maintaining your assembly

Once your assembly is deployed, you can also maintain it by issuing commands and querying various parameters related to it using the REST API. Although it is highly recommended that you use OneOps to maintain all the aspects of your deployment since it comes with robust monitoring, querying, and data gathering tools, you can also query any aspect of the assembly using the REST API, should you want to use your own scripts. The reason that you use OneOps to keep track of your deployment is because the avenues available through REST API are not as diverse as the rest of the deployment API. You can replace a component of your deployment by calling `put` on a component instance on the resource `"/<Your Organization>/assemblies/<Your assembly>/operation/environments/<Your Environment>/platforms/<Your Platform>/components/<Your Component>/instances/<Instance ID>state"`. You can again find all the details pertaining to the component and instance from the OneOps advanced GUI search. To replace the instance, you will need to pass a payload as follows:

```
{ :state => "replace" }
```

You can also get all the available actions on an instance or a component by calling get on the resource `"/<Your Organization>/assemblies>/<Your Assembley>/operation/environments/<Your Environment>/platforms/<Your Platforms>/components/<Component Name>/instances?instance_state=all"`. Finally, if you want to find all the compute instance for a platform, you can do so by running get on the resource `"/<Your Organization>/assemblies/<Your Assembly>/operation/environments/<Your Environment>/platforms/<Your Platform>/components/compute/instances.json?instance_state=all"`.

Summary

In this chapter, we touched on the tip of the iceberg that is the OneOps REST API. The OneOps REST API allows you to integrate OneOps with your own applications without logging in to OneOps. You can find a more detailed reference of the API on the OneOps documentation website. Hopefully, the sample scripts provided in this chapter stimulated you to create your own complex integrations to OneOps.

Index

www.ingramcontent.com/pod-product-compliance
Lightning Source LLC
Chambersburg PA
CBHW060534060326
40690CB00017B/3487